What others are saying about
Days of Knight

"People don't realize the type of positive impact Coach Knight has had over the years. This book not only gives a true depiction of his greatness as a coach but it also gives a true depiction of his greatness as an individual who cares about others."

—Calbert Cheaney, Indiana Hoosier, 1989–93; NBA player with the Washington Wizards, Boston Celtics, and Golden State Warriors, 1993–2006; assistant coach at St. Louis University

"I've been a fan of Kirk for a long time, going back to his high school days, when Tom Izzo and I tried to recruit him at MSU. Kirk is a person and player who has EARNED everything he's gotten out of basketball. He has always had a rare work capacity and it carried him a long, long way. He was also very hungry and humbled in his pursuit to be successful with a desire to be coached and taught. It shows up in this book."

—Coach Tom Crean, Indiana Hoosiers

"I really enjoyed this book. It was very detailed and brought back tons of memories. Fans wanting to know both the competitive and compassionate sides of Knight should definitely read *Days of Knight*."

—A. J. Guyton, Indiana Hoosier, 1996–2000 (All American, 2000); NBA player with the Chicago Bulls and Golden State Warriors, 2001–03

"I've always had the ultimate respect for Coach Knight as one of the great coaching minds of our time. When I was a young coach, he took me under his wing and provided valuable knowledge, just as he had with so many of his players. Thanks to Kirk Haston, a player I once recruited and have always appreciated, readers will gather insight as to what made Coach Knight successful, while also offering a view to a side of him that not all of us were fortunate enough to see."

—Coach Tom Izzo, Michigan State Spartans

"*Days of Knight* is a great look at how Coach Knight made the young players he coached better men first and better players second. It's a personal glimpse into how the legendary Indiana basketball coach taught and mentored his team."

—Jared Jeffries, Indiana Hoosier, 2000–2002 (member of the 2002 NCAA runner-up team); eleven-year NBA veteran, current pro personnel scout for the Denver Nuggets

"Coach Knight is a complex man with a very clear vision. Through a vast array of techniques and emotions, *Days of Knight* is an incredible inside look at Coach Knight's version of teaching the game of life and basketball. Most importantly, we see all sides of a fascinating leader and a brilliant tactician."

—Dane Fife, Indiana Hoosier, 1998–2002 (member of the 2002 NCAA runner-up team); assistant coach at Michigan State

"This is an outstanding read. Kirk has done a great job of portraying the very unique relationship that is player/coach. This book will take you inside one of the most storied college basketball programs and give you insight into one of the game's greatest coaches."

—Michael Lewis, Indiana Hoosier, 1997–2000 (IU's all-time assists leader); assistant coach at University of Nebraska

"Coach Knight stories and teachings are in the veins of Indiana—and they are in the pages of *Days of Knight*. Filled with previously unheard Knight stories and quotes, this book gives an inside look at what it was like to be a player who experienced the final three seasons of the Knight era at Indiana. If you are a Hoosier fan, you're going to want to read this book."

—Jeff Overton, Indiana Hoosier, 2002–2005; PGA Tour player; member of the 2010 U.S. Ryder Cup Team

"I've read lots of words about Bobby Knight, but never from one of his players. I can't wait to read this."

—Tony Kornheiser, co-host of ESPN's *Pardon the Interruption* and former sportswriter for the *Washington Post*

"Here's a 'Bet You Didn't Know,' Hoosier Fans: among IU's three-year-career players, only Scott May, Archie Dees, and Walt Bellamy outscored Kirk Haston; only Bellamy, Dees, and Steve Downing outrebounded him. And none of those Hoosier all-timers was blessed and cursed with the emotional peaks and valleys that Kirk went through in his IU years. . . . His mother was a school teacher, an English teacher. She would have been very proud of the excellence her son shows here as a writer, and—thanks to her urging to be a note-taker—as an inside observer of the most tumultuous years in recent IU athletics."

—Bob Hammel, author of *Knight: My Story* and *Beyond the Brink with Indiana: 1987 NCAA Champions*, and member of the Indiana Basketball Hall of Fame

"Haston paints an intense picture of what it takes to be an Indiana Hoosier and provides an inside look at the most controversial news story in IU history—the firing of Coach Bob Knight."

—Stan Sutton, author of *100 Things Hoosiers Fans Should Know and Do Before They Die*, former sportswriter for the *Courier-Journal* (Louisville), member of Indiana Sportswriters and Sportscasters Hall of Fame

To Mary,
Best Wishes to you & yours!
Go Hoosiers!

DAYS OF
KNIGHT

DAYS OF

HOW THE GENERAL CHANGED MY LIFE

KNIGHT

KIRK HASTON

INDIANA UNIVERSITY PRESS

Bloomington & Indianapolis

This book is a publication of

Indiana University Press
Office of Scholarly Publishing
Herman B Wells Library 350
1320 East 10th Street
Bloomington, Indiana 47405 USA

iupress.indiana.edu

The paper used in this publication meets the minimum requirements of
the American National Standard for Information Sciences—Permanence
of Paper for Printed Library Materials, ANSI Z39.48–1992.

Manufactured in the United States of America

Library of Congress Cataloging-in-Publication Data

Names: Haston, Kirk, 1979-
Title: Days of knight : how the general changed my life / Kirk Haston.
Description: Bloomington : Indiana University Press, [2016] |
Includes bibliographical references.
Identifiers: LCCN 2016004455 (print) | LCCN 2016030776 (ebook) |
ISBN 9780253022271 (cloth : alk. paper) | ISBN 9780253022400 (ebook)
Subjects: LCSH: Haston, Kirk, 1979- | Basketball players—United
States—Biography. | Knight, Bobby. | Basketball coaches—United States—
Biography. | Indiana University, Bloomington—Basketball.
Classification: LCC GV884.H266 A3 2016 (print) | LCC GV884.
H266 (ebook) | DDC 796.323092 [B]—dc23
LC record available at https://lccn.loc.gov/2016004455

1 2 3 4 5 21 20 19 18 17 16

small town
kid

Bob Knight
recruit

IU Hoosier
All-American

NBA Draft
1st Rd Pick

NBA Career

By Kirk Haston

Contents

Knight Lines

If you can't be ready to play every time
you put on a jersey with INDIANA on it . . .
then you can't play here.

—Coach Knight

Sophomore year, 12/1/98

Introduction

How does an eighteen-year-old from a small town in Tennessee, who went to a high school with 300 students, go to Indiana University and the Big Ten to play basketball for one of the greatest basketball coaches in the history of the game, Coach Bob Knight? It's still hard to imagine how I managed to travel down that road, and when I started there was no way I realized that my decision to be a Hoosier and play for Coach Knight would positively impact my life to such a degree. I also had no way of knowing that my first three seasons at Indiana would be the last three seasons that Knight would coach there.

My mom, Patti Kirk Haston, gave me a great gift and a terrific piece of advice when I left for Bloomington for the first time in the summer of 1997. She gave me a journal and told me, "You'll be glad someday that you wrote some things down about playing for Coach Knight." This suggestion was similar to most of the advice I received from my mom—it was absolutely correct. During my years of playing for Coach Knight I wrote down pages and pages of stories, quotes, comments, and conversations that I was fortunate enough to experience as an Indiana Hoosier. Almost every day during the season I wrote notes in my journal and also in my red notebook, a notebook that Coach Knight gave to each player and required us to have at every team meeting. From those pages of notes and from unforgettable Hoosier memories come my story and this book. The chapters follow along the timeline that took me from a high school in Lobelville, Tennessee, to Indiana University and a campus of over 35,000 students. Sprinkled throughout the book are stand-alone tales that provide a "story timeout" of sorts from the chronological action in the chapters—stories that are mostly about my experiences with Coach Knight on and off the court.

The opportunity Coach Knight gave me to play basketball at Indiana allowed me to be privy to a wide range of highs and lows in both Hoosier and college basketball history. I was on the team beginning with the 1997–98 season through the 2000–2001 season, and over those years I learned invaluable lessons about commitment, work ethic, and competition from a coaching legend. I also experienced what it was like to see that coach—the coach that my teammates and I came to play for—fired, and thus to witness the end of an era at Indiana, an era unmatched in terms of success, both on and off the court.

I've written this book for several reasons.

I want to share what it was like to be recruited by Coach Knight, as well as what it was like to practice and play for him.

I want to share how the positive far outweighs the negative when it comes to Coach Knight (in contrast to many opinions that prevail in the media, even today).

I want to share how a chubby middle-school kid made it to the NBA because a few great people believed in him and showed him how to work.

I want to share what it was like to be in the middle of the chaos that was Coach Knight's firing and Coach Mike Davis's hiring.

And last, but definitely not least, I want to share A LOT of Coach Knight stories. From the very first year I began playing for Coach Knight, until now, people from all walks of life have asked me the same question: "Do you have any Coach Knight stories?" Well, thanks to the advice and the journal Mom gave me before I became a Hoosier, I do.

1

If the Game Doesn't Fit . . .
Then You Didn't Commit

I once had the remarkable opportunity to be in the same room
with the greatest basketball winner of all time, the eleven-time
NBA champion with the Boston Celtics, Bill Russell. Of all the
great Russell quotes, my favorite is about commitment: "Commitment in my mind is [what separates] those who live their
dreams from those who live the rest of their lives regretting the
opportunities they have squandered" (quoted in Hilberg and
Falkner; see bibliography). Very early in my IU basketball career
I learned a valuable lesson about this type of commitment from
Coach Knight.

Dane Fife, Jarrod Odle, and I were the first guys to make it
downstairs into the bowels of Assembly Hall one day for practice. We made our way down the hallway to our locker room and
started to get dressed into our practice gear. As we entered our
white-walled and red-carpeted locker room, everything seemed
to be the same as usual. Our practice jerseys and shorts were
there, ready and hanging in our lockers just underneath our in-

dividualized nameplates. As we three approached our respective lockers, however, we noticed there was something very out of the ordinary about one of the upperclassmen's locker stall. I'll just call this teammate Player X. Player X's locker stall had been completely cleaned out . . . almost. His practice gear was gone, his basketball shoes were gone, all his personal effects had been cleared out, and even his nameplate had been removed from atop the locker. If it hadn't been for two conspicuous items that had been placed in this teammate's chair, his locker would have looked like it hadn't been touched all season long.

Those items were a tennis racket and a container of tennis balls.

None of us there fathomed what any of this meant. Giving Player X a call on our cell phones to see what was going on

Knight Lines

This game is not going to be fun!
If you want fun you can f_ _ _ing go outside
and swing and play on the monkey bars!
It's not fun . . . *unless* you love basketball.

—Coach Knight

Freshman year, 10/1/97

wasn't an option since there was no cell service in the lower levels of Assembly Hall. We hadn't heard any news that day about this player quitting or transferring, and that kind of news would have spread like wildfire across the Indiana University campus. My teammates and I talked a minute or two about the cleaned-out locker, but eventually headed to the basketball court to get a few shots up before the start of practice.

About half an hour later most of the players and coaches were on the court and ready to begin the day's practice, including Coach Knight. Coach was on the opposite end of the court from where the locker room entrance was located. The only player unaccounted for as the practice start time neared was Player X. I was shooting with Ted Hodges, one of the basketball managers, at an auxiliary basketball goal that was behind the baseline of the main court and in close proximity to the locker room entrance. I was shooting some close-range hook shots when Player X came out on the court through the double doors leading from the locker room.

Player X was still in his street clothes. Of course he was; he didn't have any other wardrobe options in his barren locker. As Player X made his way to the edge of the main court, the distance from which I was shooting shots also began to stretch farther and farther away from the basket. I had quickly gone from shooting low-block hook shots to shooting long-range J's from the right wing so I could get a close-up look at the inevitable showdown that was going to take place between Player X and Coach Knight. Player X was now standing on the sideline of the main court. He just stood there for several seconds, staring toward Coach Knight, who was still at the opposite end of the court talking with his assistant coaches. Player X wasn't empty-handed as he stood at the edge of the basketball court. He was holding the tennis balls and racket that had been left in his locker. Suddenly, over all the sneaker squeaking and ball bouncing, Player X shouted in the direction of Coach Knight: *"Hey Coach, what's this about*!?!" Assembly Hall fell silent. Now was the time for the showdown. I could have sworn I saw a Wild West tumbleweed roll across half-court as Coach Knight turned and looked in the direction of Player X.

Coach Knight didn't say a word, or even change expressions. As he began the ninety-four-foot walk toward his disgruntled player, all the rest of us pretended to go back to what we were doing, though we were completely focused on the face-to-face meeting about to occur. Player X hadn't moved one step closer or further away as Coach Knight came to a stop two feet in front of him. Coach Knight spoke first and last. He didn't raise his voice; he didn't even point a finger. He just simply answered the question that had just been shouted at him from across the court. *"You've shown you aren't committed to playing a team sport, so I thought you'd be better off taking up an individual sport instead. Now go on home."*

Coach Knight wasn't talking about the "home" that was his apartment in Bloomington; he meant for him to get out of town and go to his *real* home. Player X didn't say a word back, but just turned, exited the court, and left Assembly Hall.

It didn't take me long once I got to IU to realize what commitment *really* meant. Playing basketball for Coach Knight required a level of commitment to work, to preparation, and to competition that could push you past your previous physical and mental limits and toward goals that you didn't even know were possible.

Crazy Brave

In August 1998, Coach Knight had just gotten back from visiting his good friend Tony LaRussa, then the manager of the St. Louis Cardinals. While Coach was in St. Louis, he watched the Cardinals play the Atlanta Braves. Coach Knight would often come back from such trips and tell us a story or two in the locker room after *good* practices—when he was usually in a good mood. This day he told us about the players he had talked with on this trip as he visited the Cardinals' and Braves' clubhouses.

Coach said he overheard a high-salaried player in the Cardinals' clubhouse complaining about the workload they were still carrying in practice, something to the effect of "When are they going to call up those minor leaguers so they can do this stuff instead?" There are few things Coach Knight detests more than a player who limits his own potential by not embracing the process of work.

The Braves' clubhouse, he said, "felt more like the championship [Cincinnati] Reds teams" he used to visit, the Bench–Morgan–Rose "Big Red Machine" teams of the 1970s. Coach said his primary reason for stopping by the Braves clubhouse was to talk with future Hall of Fame pitcher Greg Maddux. Coach told us how much he respected Maddux's game because of his detailed, intellectual approach to preparation.

Knight Lines

There's a greater chance of Madonna regaining her virginity than you using your [off] hand!

—Coach Knight

Freshman year, 10/97

Once Coach entered the Braves' clubhouse, it didn't take long for some of the big names of the Braves to find their way over to talk to "The General."

First up was Cy Young Award winner and eight-time All-Star John Smoltz, an avid sports fan who stayed current on several sports, one of them definitely being college basketball. He had been not only a top pitching prospect but also an all-state high school basketball player in Michigan, with a scholarship offer to play basketball for the Michigan State Spartans. Although he wisely chose baseball and never attended MSU, he was a big fan of the school's basketball program. So Smoltz had some fun: he came over to razz Coach Knight a little about some recent Michigan State and Indiana battles on the basketball court.

Tom Glavine was to be that day's starting pitcher about an hour and a half later, but he still made a point to come over to shake Coach Knight's hand, just before one of his Braves teammates, Chipper Jones, made an extremely dramatic move to get Coach Knight's attention. Instead of just going with the usual handshake, Jones chose to throw a chair toward Coach Knight—and this was the first time he had ever met him. As you can imagine, the whole locker room froze. What was going to happen next? Ever since Coach Knight had thrown one chair in one game in 1985 he had held the crown as the most famous chair thrower in sports history. It appeared that Chipper Jones had decided to use this moment with Coach Knight to stake his own claim for the title. Without raising his voice, however, Coach, turning to Smoltz, Maddux, and Glavine, broke the silence in the room by asking, "How old is Jones? 25, 26? D _ _ N! He only threw that chair across the room? I'm two times his age and I can put it through that wall!"

2

Tennessee Knight Game

*L*ooking back at what the recruiting process was like for me in high school, it's amazing how close I came to *not* going to Indiana University to play basketball. To start with, I was about as close as you can get to never even being *recruited* by IU. Halfway through my junior year at Perry County High School in Tennessee, I was 6'9" and 220 pounds. I was being recruited by Ohio State, Vanderbilt, Tennessee, and Purdue (all of whom would eventually offer scholarships by my senior year). Everyone knew Coach Knight's recruiting focus at IU was usually on players from Indiana, Illinois, and Ohio, so I felt far off IU's radar during the bulk of my high school playing days. My first encounter with Coach Knight really wasn't one at all. The summer before my senior year, we were both at a team camp in Memphis called the Steamboat Shootout. Our "encounter" lasted about ten seconds; he walked right past me in the doorway of the gym where my high school team was getting ready to play—not past me going into the gym to watch our game, but going *out* of the gym after he had evaluated another player.

Knight Lines

I'm not going to recruit anymore kids that are *supposed* to be great or have a lot of "potential." *Potential* is the most f_ _ _ ing overused and misunderstood word in history!

—Coach Knight

Freshman year, 9/21/97

I wasn't offended. At the time I had absolutely no interest and no intention of leaving my home state to play basketball. I guess it would be fair to say that I really wasn't too big a fan of leaving home for much of anything in those days. Two main towns make up Perry County, which has a total population of about 8,000. My hometown of Lobelville (3,000) is the smaller of the two towns. The other, Linden, is the county seat and site of the county's only high school, Perry County High. There has always been a friendly (and sometimes not so friendly) small-town vs. smaller-town rivalry between Linden and Lobelville. However, since students from both towns' middle schools feed into the same high school to play for the Vikings, it can make you feel like you're less from a hometown and more from a home county. As a junior in high school, I loved being close to home so much that it affected my approach to the recruiting process. If I deemed a school too far from home, I automatically crossed that school off my list. Looking back now, I was incredibly short-sighted and weak-minded in limiting my options so drastically for fear of feeling a little homesick.

Like me, my mom was an only child, which meant our immediate family was a pretty small group. My father left when I was four because of some personal problems he was struggling to overcome. Because of this, most of my childhood family moments included three people: my mom, Patti Kirk Haston, and her parents, Hoyt and Bettye Kirk. We did have a good-size extended family in Perry County, thanks to the close connections we had through Lobelville Elementary, the school where my mom was a fifth-grade teacher, and through the Linden Church of Christ, where my granddad preached. But by far the most influential people in my life were Mom, my granny, and my granddad. It's great to feel comfort and support from your family, but that feeling can be *so* comforting to a kid that it makes the unknowns and unfamiliarity of distance seem an intimidating obstacle to overcome. Unsurprisingly, the two teams at the top of my college basketball wish list were two in-state schools, Vanderbilt and Tennessee.

By the start of my senior year I had been offered basketball scholarships from both. At the time I thought that this whole recruiting process was a piece of cake. I wanted to stay close to home, and I wanted to sign early. So in the fall of my senior year, with the early signing date quickly approaching, everything seemed perfectly in place. Vanderbilt was less than two hours away, so signing with Vanderbilt seemed a no-brainer to me. I was less certain of my backup plan involving Tennessee, mainly because of the distance from home to Knoxville, but since I wanted to stay in-state, UT was still solidly my second choice.

One slight problem developed. Vanderbilt and Tennessee both reneged on their scholarship offers to me.

Vanderbilt's head basketball coach at that time was Jan van Breda Kolff (whom I'll shortcut to JVBK from here on out). JVBK had been actively recruiting me during my junior year, but by the time the early signing period had arrived, his interest in me inexplicably dried up. I really don't know why, but he stopped recruiting me altogether. Then, after a phone call from my high school coach, Bruce Slatten, to the Volunteer coaching staff, I found out I wouldn't be heading to Knoxville, either. Kevin O'Neill, the UT head coach, called me later to explain that they still wanted me there, but that they no longer had a scholarship available to offer since they had a rush of recruits commit early.

Very suddenly, I was now officially being *un*-recruited. After a year of going through the recruiting process I suddenly found myself back to square one. I had some other scholarship offers on the table but none really intrigued me, so I chose to wait for the late signing period in April. I hoped my team and I would have a strong season and this might draw some new recruiting interest. Reality had forced me to realize that my two in-state safety nets were gone. It was time to focus solely on finding a coach who would push me to reach my potential as a basketball player, wherever he and his school were.

The first half of my senior season went smoothly. We were 16–0 and ranked no. 1 in Class A (the smallest of Tennessee's three divisions, though Coach Slatten filled most of our schedule with teams from the two larger divisions, Class AA and AAA). I was averaging 20 points, 12 rebounds, and 4 blocks per game. And this was when I got the chance to meet the Indiana Hoosiers' head basketball coach—well, actually, their future coach, Tom Crean. Michigan State's head coach, Tom Izzo, dispatched Coach Crean, his assistant, to watch one of our practices. He was the first coach from the Big Ten to come to Tennessee to watch me play or practice. By the midway point of our season, Purdue, Ohio State, and Michigan State made up my short list of schools. Surprisingly, another coach jumped back into the recruiting mix around this time: Vanderbilt's JVBK. Coach Slatten told me JVBK called him, saying that he was again interested in signing me to play for the Commodores and that one of the reasons for this renewed recruiting interest was because some Vanderbilt backers wanted him to bring more in-state talent to Vandy's campus. I didn't find that the most convincing recruiting sales pitch of all-time. I passed on playing for Mr. Jan.

As our Christmas/New Year's Day holiday break came and went, my potential college options seemed locked in, and I thought it best to make a choice and commit to a school before we got into tournament play in February. In mid-January, however, Coach Slatten got a call from Bloomington, Indiana, which changed everything. He called me to his office in between classes to give me the news: Coach Bob Knight was interested in taking a look at me. In all honesty, I thought he was joking. As he related the details about how Coach Knight wanted to look at some game tapes and how an assistant coach from Indiana University was going to come down to one of our practices, it hit me that this was not a joke at all. It was a stretch to say at that point that the Indiana Hoosiers were recruiting me. They were more or less just doing their due diligence to determine whether or not they wanted to *begin* the recruiting process with me. I found out later that it was actually a tip from another college's head coach that had precipitated this interest from the Hoosiers—a friend-to-friend call to Coach Knight from Tennessee's Kevin O'Neill. He told Coach Knight he might want to take a look at a Tennessee kid they had wanted to sign but couldn't for lack of available scholarships.

I couldn't wait to tell my granddad. On hearing the news that Coach Knight had called about me, my granddad (the minister) simply replied, "He sure does cuss a lot."

As I arrived at school on the morning of January 28, 1997, my feelings ranged somewhere between (A) wanting to shadowbox around the gym to the theme music from *Rocky IV* and (B) wanting to lie down in the fetal position at half-court. All this was because of the road game we would be playing later that night at Clifton High School. Sure, it was a district game and our undefeated 21–0 record would be on the line, but neither of these reasons had to do with my eagerness. The Clifton Lions were a team we had beaten fairly easily earlier in the season, and if our team played anywhere near our capabilities, we would win again. My excitement was because Coach Knight himself was planning to fly from Indiana that night to watch me play. It had been a big deal to me that he had sent an assistant down to watch me practice, but a visit from Coach Knight himself was at a different level all together. Basketball players have a pretty common basketball pregame ritual that has been passed down from generation to generation. I believe it may have been my Hoosier teammate Tom Coverdale that gave this ritual an inelegant but apt title: "A nap and a crap." Well, let's just say that on this particular game day my body didn't really want to cooperate on either one of these fronts.

I had known for a couple of days that Coach Knight had planned to see our game at Clifton, but I had barely told anyone about it—just my family and, on the night of the game, two teammates, my best friend, Chad Marrs, and our team's point guard, Cory Brown. Coach Slatten said it would be best for us to keep Coach Knight's recruiting visit quiet in case he had to cancel his trip at the last minute (a distinct possibility for someone as busy as Coach Knight in the middle of the Big Ten basketball season). Sitting on this kind of basketball news in a place like Perry County was brutal. His visit would make this game a huge event in our basketball-crazed area. Coach Knight, the 1984 U.S. Olympic coach, would be the first head coach to personally come to one of our games that season. This was overwhelming to me. Coach Knight was personally coming to Tennessee to watch me play so he could decide for himself if I was a player he wanted to recruit to IU.

It was hard to believe. This was someone who, not long before, had coached his team to a victory in the preseason NIT finals versus Duke at Madison Square Garden in New York. Now, he was supposed to be in little Clifton, Tennessee, to watch a high school game in the smallest and oldest gym in our district.

We normally had a good traveling fan base for road games, especially with our undefeated record. For this game, however, there were two factors that would considerably reduce the number of our fans coming to see us play: it was a weeknight game and it was against an opponent we had already beaten by double digits earlier in the season. So here was a road game many of them wouldn't attend that could end up being the one road game none of them would have wanted to miss.

In Tennessee, the girls' basketball games precede the boys' games. I was usually the first guy on our team who went to the locker room, usually near the end of the first quarter of the girls' game. I would get dressed, stretch, and maybe listen to some Hootie and the Blowfish on my portable CD player. On this night, though, I stayed seated in Clifton's old-school, wood bleachers just a little longer than normal so I could keep an eye on the gym's one main entrance: underneath the goal nearest the end of the court where the Clifton Lions' bench was located. I was still there in the second quarter, giving myself some extra time to spot Coach Knight's arrival, but I never did see him. So I headed down to our locker room with a growing feeling of disappointment welling up in the pit of my stomach. I didn't see Coach Knight anywhere, but I did notice something else in the bleachers: a lack of people sitting in them.

The rest of my teammates came down to get dressed at halftime or a couple of minutes into the third quarter of the girls' game. As Chad and Cory entered the locker room I looked up at them from where I was stretching, hoping that a look on one of their faces might indicate they had just seen Coach Knight arrive in the gymnasium. But as they and the rest of the team filed into the small locker room, no one gave any indication that they had seen anything out of the ordinary. I remembered that when I woke up that morning, I thought it could be one of the most important days of my life, but as we lined up to take the court for warm-ups, it felt much closer to one of the most disappointing days instead.

The scoreboard clock began to tick down from 15:00. We ran out and started two layup lines on the end of the court nearest the gym's main entrance. Our layup line was proceeding as it always did at the start of warm-ups when suddenly the entire atmosphere of the Clifton High School gymnasium changed. The normal sounds of balls bouncing and shoes squeaking were suddenly drowned out by a chattering buzz of conversations in the bleachers and lobby. I knew exactly what this meant before any of my teammates could figure it out. Coach Knight was in the building! I hadn't seen him yet (oddly enough, I didn't seem him the whole night). The first sighting confirmation that I got during warm-ups came from a good friend of mine, Blake. Now I was full of nervous energy and doing my best to stay focused on the important audition I was going to have as soon as warm-ups concluded. However, these circumstances didn't stop my bud Blake from enjoying himself. Every time he passed by me in our layup lines, he would utter, "Ohhhhh, Bobby Knight is here to watch you tonight—no pressure!" or "Knight is gonna be watchin', so you better not suck tonight!" I knew this was all said in good fun, but if it wouldn't have given Coach Knight such a bad first impression, I might have beaned Blake in the back of the head with a basketball.

Never before had I felt equally relieved and anxious at the same time. I was thrilled that Coach Knight had made it to our game, but my heart was racing as we neared tipoff. As both teams continued with warm-ups, I noticed people were constantly speed walking, some even jogging, in and out of the main lobby of the gym. This was a little confusing. I knew they couldn't be going out to the lobby to see or try to meet Coach Knight because we were close enough to tip-off that he had surely found his way to a seat somewhere by now. What I found out later was that Perry County and Clifton folks alike—at a time when having a cell phone was a rarity—were lining up to use the payphones, or any other phone that the school would let them use, to call friends and family and inform them what was going on at the gym at Clifton High School and that they should get out there ASAP! After what felt like an extremely long warm-up time, the game was finally set to begin (I think the scoreboard operator may have tacked a couple of extra minutes onto the warm-up time to give people who had just found out about Coach Knight's presence some extra time to get to the game). Coach Slatten called a set lob play called "Gold 2" on our first offensive possession. It worked perfectly. I caught a textbook lob pass from Cory along the right baseline and finished the play, opening the game with a two-handed dunk that brought a nice reaction from the fans in the stands—which by now were almost completely filled.

The first half went well. We got out to a nice 15-point lead in the first quarter and pushed it to 23 by halftime. I knocked down some 10–15 foot jumpers, got a couple of jump hooks to go down, and grabbed more than a few rebounds, but since we weren't playing the strongest of competition I just didn't know if I was playing in a way that would impress a man of Coach Knight's stature. Right after the game I was eager to meet and talk with him for the first time and maybe get a sense of whether he was still interested in recruiting me. These thoughts were quickly dashed in the locker room, however, when Coach Slatten informed me that Coach Knight had left the game at halftime and headed back to the airport. My heart sank. Coach Slatten didn't have any other information, so that's all I had to go on for the rest of the night and into the next day.

Knight Lines

Running into a screen is like a guy taking a nap under a tree and having a cow come by and p_ _ _ing on his head and not waking up.

—Coach Knight

Junior year, 11/28/99

It's Not Business, It's Personal

When it comes to movie actors, Coach Knight always seemed to be more of a John Wayne or George C. Scott kind of guy rather than an Al Pacino type. So it was no surprise that his motto was a far cry from Michael Corleone's "It's not personal . . . it's strictly business" motto in *The Godfather*. As a matter of fact, I would say that Coach Knight was strictly in the business of taking things personally! This was probably one of the reasons that he was able to push himself to such great achievements (and also to great frustrations at times). This character trait of taking everything personally can be found in other all-time greats as well. Larry Bird was of course a legend for his basketball talents, but his on-court trash talk and personal dislike for opponents was equally legendary. Anyone who has watched the ESPN 30 for 30 *Bad Boys* film knows that Isiah Thomas (and the entire Detroit Pistons in the late 1980s and early 1990s, for that matter) took every look, gesture, and comment so personally that often their games ended up leading to fistfights. And, of course, the most noteworthy "chip on the shoulder" superstar is Michael Jordan, who allegedly went so far as to make up trash talk that opponents had *never even said* about him just so he could get motivated to score another fifty points on some poor, unsuspecting Eastern Conference shooting guard. Coach Knight was definitely in this same category of competitor as the legends listed above.

In one game at Indiana I suffered an injury to my leg in the first half while trying to keep the player I was defending from getting good post position. It was nothing serious, but it was enough of an injury that the doctors needed me to go back to the training room so they could further examine my leg during halftime. The first half of this particular game had not gone well for us and we were down by double digits. I was still lying down on an examining table in the training room adjacent to the locker room when my teammates and the coaching staff entered. I couldn't see into the locker room from where we were in the training room, but I definitely could hear everything that Coach Knight said in his halftime speech. Coach didn't hold back as he quickly detailed in eviscerating fashion how pitiful an effort we had given on the court in the first 20 minutes of play, adding that if we didn't change our attitude we were going to continue to get embarrassed by our opponent. I can still to this day remember exactly what I was thinking while I was in the training room getting checked: "I am soooo glad I'm not in that locker room at this very moment." I was by no means glad that I was dealing with an injury, but in the short term I was thinking, "Hey, at least I dodged that butt-chewing in the other room."

Coach Knight gave his final marching orders and halftime adjustments to my teammates and sent them back out to the court to warm up for the second half. As the team departed the locker room, the door of the training room swung open and Coach Knight walked in and approached the table. I remember think-

Knight Lines

Take criticism personally
and *then* do something about it!

—Coach Knight

Sophomore year, 2/21/99

ing as Coach Knight slowly approached, "This is nice of Coach to come in and check on how I'm doing." Just as that thought went through my mind Coach Knight said, "*You know, if you learned to play defense the right way you wouldn't have gotten hurt.*" This wasn't said with any maliciousness, just in a matter-of-fact manner. A minor injury wasn't a free pass for me to dodge Coach's critique. Sure, after the game he showed plenty of concern for my injury, but halftime of a heated basketball game was no time for sympathy, only for coaching.

Coach never held back what he thought. This was especially true when it came to talking about rival coaches, rival teams, and disappointing team efforts. Here are a few comments that I jotted down in my red notebook that all could be placed in the "not business" file:

> *"All in one season, this team is among one of my all-time favorites . . . and one of my most hated!"* 2/24/00

> *"Totally f_ _ _ ing inexcusable the way we played against Purdue!"* 2/13/99

"The worst thing is to see you not succeed. Go away somewhere in the country and be coached by someone who won't get on your a_ s!" 1/22/00

"I can't bench everybody!" 3/7/00

"Mistakes equal a selfish player." 10/18/99

"[Major D1 coach] just got a job next year at Southern Catholic University for Women . . . I guess they'll suck next year." 3/8/00

*"*FIFE*! Lewis is burning your a_ s! Someone turn the sprinklers on Fife's a_s!"* 98–99

"We got 23 wins last year on horse s_ _ t defense!" 11/6/99

"You can average 25 points a game and [still] be a sh_ _ _ y player!" 11/21/98

"I work too hard to be disgraced by this type of play this morning!" 12/19/98

"We can't win 1 game out of the next 6 with your defense!" 2/11/00

"I want a player who wants the team to be the best!" 8/29/98

"Kids today aren't focused on what's important in the game. Focus on screening, setting up cuts, and playing as a team." 2/24/99

"We've had some first-class b_ _ _ _ ers and complainers!"
8/29/98

"We've had 120 days of work leading up to last night's
game and we lost it in the first five minutes! Be back here
ready to practice at 5:30 AM tomorrow." 2/10/99

This team could be 17–0 with a heartbeat of effort!"
1/22/00

"Everyone [in this room] has a beat a_ s." 12/11/98 (before
practice in Assembly Hall, following a loss to Kentucky)

"Some of you have already forgotten about the [loss]. Other
teams have wanted to learn how to win! This season is
almost lost. We're right on the brink of that." 2/11/99

"You embarrassed yourself last night!" 1/6/99

"More games are lost by good [players] than won by poor
[players]." 12/27/98

"[Kirk] doesn't need any female attention . . . he needs a
kick in the a_ s!" 3/8/00

"It's like a court case. We know they're guilty, we just gotta
go prove it. We know we're a better team, [so] let's go prove
it!" 2/4/00

"If we are going to be good, we have to play thinking about
how we play and not **who** we play." 12/10/99

"I've lost 281 games before Saturday night. [Know] why one more loss makes a difference? Because losing is not acceptable to me!" 12/14/99

"[Always] make plays that you would make when one point behind or one point ahead." 12/26/98

"Someone fell asleep yesterday [in the Temple game], who was it? [Coach Knight stares right at me]. *First Kirk, you let [your man] get free for a wide-open dunk and then [he] misses the dunk. Both of you are dumb as hell!"* 12/7/98

"We're flat-a_ s better than Purdue!" 2/9/99

3

The Day after Knight

*A*lthough my stats were pretty good in the game versus Clifton, I knew by this point that it wasn't just numbers that a college coach looks at when evaluating talent. There are a lot of areas in a player's game that a coach wants to see with his own eyes. If it were only about numbers, coaches could just look at stat sheets and offer scholarships to the kids averaging the most points, rebounds, and assists. A college coach wants to see how you run the floor, catch a pass, make a pass, how you work within the offense, how you position yourself for rebounds, and how you see the floor—things that don't necessarily show up in a stat line at the end of a game. I wanted to know what Coach Knight had thought. I talked to Coach Slatten later that evening to see if he had any other information to share with me, good or bad, concerning Coach Knight's visit. He told me we would hear something from IU's staff sometime the next day about their level of recruiting interest. Needless to say, a peaceful night of sleep evaded me that evening when I got home.

The next morning I couldn't wait to get to school. I was hoping Coach Slatten had already received a phone call from

Coach Knight, and I would find out something as soon as I got to school. When I arrived, I went straight to the gym to see once again if Coach Slatten had heard anything yet from IU. My visit to his office didn't take long; he still hadn't heard anything. The first-period bell was just moments away from ringing. As I turned to head to my class, Coach Slatten told me that as soon as he heard anything he would let me know. Focusing on math equations, world history, and *The Great Gatsby* was going to be a rather difficult task on this day.

Coach Slatten finally came to my fifth-period English class to get me. I walked down the hallway with him into the principal's office. There, lying on the desk, was a phone that was off the hook, waiting for me to pick up. Coach Slatten motioned me toward the phone but told me nothing about who was on the line, just that the caller was from IU. As I picked up the phone, Coach Slatten and the principal stepped outside the office and shut the door. "Hello," I said, having no idea whom I was addressing.

"Kirk, this is Coach Knight. I want you to come play for us. How does that sound?"

I could have really, really used a glass of water at that moment. My mouth went dry as my mind tried to process the meaning of the first three sentences Coach Knight had ever spoken to me.

Knight Lines

One day you'll be d_ _n glad you crossed my path!

—Coach Knight

Freshman year, 2/23/98

He had begun our talk on the phone like he and I had been in the middle of a twenty-minute conversation (which I later came to realize was often the norm when it came to phone conversations with Coach Knight). Skip the pleasantries, skip the small talk, and just get right to the point. Three weeks ago, I was excited about the prospects of IU wanting to take a look at me, and one minute ago I would have been glad to hear that the Hoosiers were still interested enough to take the next step in the recruiting process, like taking a visit to Bloomington or sending an assistant to another game later in the season. Wow! This scenario was unexpected. I didn't just have some assistant coach telling me, "We may have a spot for you here at Fill-in-the-Blank University." I had a legendary coach telling me that he wanted me to play for him. Without hesitation, the next words out of my mouth were, "Coach, if you think I can play for you, then I want to go to Indiana." Coach Knight told me that some people from IU would be getting in touch with us and then the call was over. I had no idea at the time that this short talk would eventually lead to a multitude of lessons learned and opportunities opened. I had just had a two-minute conversation that would forever change my life for the better.

And just like that, the recruiting experience was finally over. I came out of the office and told Coach Slatten I was going to be a Hoosier. It was quite a relief for both him and me that the recruiting process was now over. I could tell he was proud that all our work had finally culminated in a commitment to an incredible coach and school. Coach Slatten had put in a great deal of time helping me with my game and assisting me in getting noticed by college scouts. He said he was going to keep the news quiet until I had a chance to make a few important phone calls. I called my mom, my granddad and granny, and a close friend of mine, Hollis Hinson, to let them all know of the decision I had made. The memory I have from making those phone calls was just the joy they all had because I had found a school to play for that I was both excited and confident about. I could tell Mom was excited about my decision, but her reaction was a bit on the subdued side as she told me, "Son, if that's where you want to go, then I am behind you and I'm proud of you." I think it had already started to set in for my mom that her only child was going to be moving 350 miles away from home in the near future.

One phone number that I wasn't excited about dialing had a West Lafayette, Indiana, area code. I had a scholarship offer on the table from the other Big Ten school in Indiana, Purdue University. I finally got up the nerve to call Coach Gene Keady, the longtime Purdue Boilermakers' head coach, and a longtime rival of Coach Knight and the Hoosiers. It's never easy to inform any coach that you are turning down his scholarship offer, but it was going to be especially difficult for me to tell this to a coach when it involved his school's hated in-state rival. Once I got Coach Keady on the phone I informed him that I would be heading to Bloomington to play basketball. I'll never forget what he said next: "That's fine, Kirk, but just know from this point on . . . I'm gonna root like hell against you."

Recruiting Trip

With my college decision behind me, the rest of my senior year went as well as I could have ever hoped. We redeemed our state championship loss the season before by coming out in the 1996–97 season and winning every single game we played, finishing with a record of 37–0. We won the TSSAA Class A state championship by winning our quarterfinal game against Chattanooga Christian by 30 points, beating Upperman in our semifinal game by 25 points, and then defeating the Columbia Academy Bulldogs (one of our top rivals) in the championship game, 82–47.

Knight Lines

Kirk, I didn't go down to Podunk, Tennessee, and bring you up here to *NOT* play defense!

—Coach Knight

Junior year, 1999

After all the celebrating had ended in Perry County, Tennessee, it was time to focus my attention on Monroe County, Indiana.

I committed to Indiana without ever taking a recruiting visit, which is why I thought that it would probably be a good idea to take a little trip to Bloomington during the latter part of my senior year. A few weeks after our final state tournament game I made the northern trek for an official recruiting visit to Indiana University. Upon arriving in Bloomington I was picked up by Ron Felling, one of Coach Knight's assistant coaches at the time, who took me to the apartment I would be staying at for the next couple of days.

The apartment I stayed at was Mike Lewis's and the late Jason Collier's. In 2015, I played golf with Michael Lewis at an Indiana basketball reunion, and part of the conversation that afternoon was about this very recruiting visit. Lewis told me, "You were the easiest recruit we ever hosted. We asked if you wanted to go out anywhere and you just said you were fine hanging out at the apartment. So Jason and I just went and picked you up some food at BuffaLouie's and called it a day." I said that it was probably a good thing that I had already committed before I came there because their apartment probably wasn't the most sanitary recruiting tool the Hoosiers basketball program had in their arsenal. All in all, though, they did a good job selling the basketball program to me, and also did a fine job picking out wings and sandwiches at BuffaLouie's.

During one of my meetings with Coach Knight during the recruiting trip, he told me how he had come to the decision to offer me a scholarship to play at Indiana. At the high school game of mine that he had attended in Clifton, Coach had brought along his wife, Karen. He told me that she had been a successful coach in her own right, an Oklahoma Girls Basketball Hall of Famer, as a matter of fact. Coach went on to say,

> *I was looking at two kids for one scholarship we had remaining. It was between you and another post player we'd been looking at. Karen had seen both of you play, so that night when we were leaving your game I turned to her and asked, "So which one of these kids do you think I should go after?" She told me that I should go with "the Tennessee kid."*

I had been through many recruiting visits from assistant coaches, opened hundreds of recruiting letters, and played in dozens of basketball camps and AAU tournaments during the recruiting process—yet it was the advice of a head coach's wife that would forever change my fate.

Thanks, Ms. Karen, for saying "the Tennessee kid."

4

Welcome to B-Town Greenhorn

*I*t was very appropriate that my first experience upon moving to Bloomington in the summer of 1997 was working at the Hoosiers' youth basketball camp, which was named the Bob Knight Basketball School. All the current Hoosier players worked as counselors at the camp, while the incoming freshmen worked the concession stand that was set up outside between the two dormitories where the kids attending the camp stayed. So for most of the day during camp week, from 9 AM to 7 PM, Dane Fife, Jarrod Odle, Luke Recker, Tom Geyer, and I sat outside at a couple of tables and sold drinks, snacks, and slice after slice after slice of Papa John's pizza (I myself ate so much Papa John's pizza that to this day I haven't had another slice). We did get about a ninety-minute lunch break, but an hour of that was spent at our daily weightlifting session in Assembly Hall. They were long days, but I enjoyed getting to know the guys I would be working and playing with over the next few years. It was fitting that the very first lesson I would learn while on Indiana University's campus happened at the Bob Knight Basketball School camp.

Ironically, though, it wouldn't be taught by Coach Knight, but by a future Super Bowl champion.

Along with the rest of the new guys on campus, there was one more incoming basketball freshman selling Snickers bars that week who was also planning on playing a little football while he was at Indiana. This fellow freshman was Antwaan Randle El, future Pittsburgh Steelers wide receiver (and Indiana University Hall of Famer). Randle El was an intelligent, to-the-point guy who spoke in a cadence that mirrored his darty quickness on the basketball court and on the football field. Antwaan never shied away from a challenge on the field and wasn't a bit shy about giving his opinion off the field, either. During Antwaan's time with the basketball team he and Coach Knight shared some classic exchanges, which Coach Knight seemed to thoroughly enjoy. One such banter came during a friendly debate the team was having with Coach Knight about the possibility of changing from Converse shoes to either Nike or Reebok. As quickly as Coach Knight could fire questions at us about why we should switch, Antwaan would return fire with sharp responses. Antwaan was trying his best to argue that Converse's shoes were heavier than both Nike and Reebok, while Coach would counter that there wasn't much difference between the three. Coach finally paused and looked at Antwaan and said, "*You're an opinionated little guy, aren't you?*" Antwaan, finally silenced for a moment, simply looked back at Coach Knight with a half-smirk on his face. "*What's wrong?*" Coach asked. "*Am I lying? Are you opinionated?*" Antwaan nodded his head in agreement. "*Are you a little guy?*" "Yes," replied Antwaan. "*Then I wasn't lying and you can't say anything.*" It was probably one of the few times that Coach Knight was able to get the last word in against the future Steelers wideout. The next day Coach Knight showed up in the locker room armed with data. He had sent a manager to a local shoe store with our team's Converse sneakers. He had instructed the manager to have the Converse pair weighed against a pair of Nike and Reebok sneakers. Coach Knight looked down at the note card in his hand and now, with his own half-smirk, read it aloud to the entire team—but specifically to Antwaan: "*Reebok, 1 pound and 6 ounces. Nike, 1 pound and 6 ounces. Converse, 1 pound and 7 ounces.*"

We had all been on campus for less than a week before Antwaan fired one of his opinions in my direction: "Kirk, I've got two pieces of advice for you. Go buy a belt and an iron." Thanks, Antwaan, like I didn't have enough on my mind to worry about. I was already trying to deal with living in a town that was further from home than many of the vacations my family took when I was growing up. Getting adjusted to life in Bloomington was definitely going to take some time. I knew I had some weaknesses that I had to improve on before I could succeed in the classroom and on the court as a newly minted Hoosier. Luckily, though, I could at least take care of a couple of my weak spots immediately. That evening I drove to Target and bought a belt and an iron.

In those early days of my freshman year, I was in need of all the advice I could get. It was quite an adjustment to go from high school classes connected by hallways that could be measured in feet to college classes that were sometimes separated by miles. Something else that was a shock to my system was the sheer number of students that were enrolled on campus— around 35,000. In the first college class I ever attended, I walked into a lecture hall and found more students in that one class than had been enrolled in my entire high school the preceding year. Getting used to the size of the Bloomington campus was just one of the many "new normals" of my freshman year at IU. But the toughest of these adjustments was getting used to Coach Knight's workouts and practices.

I was terrified of not being prepared or up to the challenge of the workouts and practices that were quickly approaching. I

Knight Lines

Kirk, you're a babe in the woods right now.

—Coach Knight
Freshman year, 9/1/97

had heard all the "Knight-mare" stories from the upperclassmen about how demanding the basketball practices and strength and conditioning workouts were. I had already heard Coach Knight comically explaining how a couple of these very upperclassmen on our team had not been as prepared for practices in the past as they should have been: *"If you robbed a bank you'd walk in with two guns in your hand but be so dumb you'd put them down so you could write the teller a check, then turn around to see five cops with machine guns ready to turn you into Swiss cheese."*

My first taste of playing for Coach Knight at Indiana came during the weeks of our individual workouts that preceded team practices, which began in mid-October. These workouts would have a maximum of four players at a time on the court, and were limited to forty-five minutes. Coach Knight had his assistant coaches, Mike Davis, John Treloar, and Pat Knight, run the basketball drills for these preseason sessions. I had no idea what I was in for going into my first individual workout. I felt I had worked hard at basketball drills in high school. So, as my first-ever Hoosier individual workout approached, I wasn't really buying into all the hype that my upperclassmen teammates were trying to sell me about the difficulty of these forty-five-minute sessions.

Well, I may not have been buying the hype beforehand, but I sure was after my workout—along with some Advil and Icy Hot.

All the players dressed the same for the individual workouts. We had our white and red Converse sneakers, along with our red shorts and a solid gray, short-sleeve T-shirt. (Before I get a bunch of tweets from Hoosier fans informing me that Hoosier colors are cream and crimson, let me explain: Coach Knight always called our teams in practice the "white team" and the "red team," so we usually used those terms when describing our colors as well.) If there was a group working out before your group, you waited outside closed double doors nearest the training room. Players would wait there until they got the go-ahead to enter, usually from one of our fifteen managers who were always at the individual workouts.

Those few minutes waiting outside the doors for your group's workout to begin were always agonizing. The only sounds you could hear were of basketballs bouncing, sneakers violently squeaking on the Assembly Hall hardwood, and coaches yelling to go quicker, faster, and harder. If that alone wasn't enough to get your stomach churning for what was about to take place in the next forty-five minutes of your life, the double doors would then open to give you a glimpse into your future.

Knight Lines

I hate guys who think they can become good by half-a_ sing it, by just showing up . . . you have to work hard to become good!

—Coach Knight

Freshman year, 10/1/97

Emerging from the bright lights of the Assembly Hall court and into the dark corridor where we were waiting were the four players who had just finished their workouts, without a dry inch to be found on their sweat-soaked gray T-shirts. I always found myself a bit jealous of the guys who had just completed their individual workouts and were headed to the oasis of the training room. My group was just getting ready to enter the gym where defensive slides and passing-lane denial drills awaited. Meanwhile, they were heading into the training room where cold Gatorade and ice bags awaited. Usually the group that had just finished with their workout would walk past the four waiting players with barely a look or nod of acknowledgment; they would use whatever energy they had left just to put one foot in front of the other. However, there was always one teammate who would nevertheless muster the energy to greet the incoming group of players, and that was Michael Lewis, the all-time Hoosiers assist leader and currently an assistant coach at Butler. Lewis was always good for a Grinch-like grin along with a "good luck with *that* workout" comment that was part antagonistic sarcasm and part relief for being finished with his own workout for the day.

One of the main things I remember about our individual workouts was that there was hardly a minute of down time, and yes, I literally mean one minute. Coach Knight and his assistant coaches had the drill rotations down to a fine art. For instance, each of the fifteen managers knew exactly where they were to be stationed for each of the drills. The managers were a crucial part of the efficiency of these individual workouts (and a crucial part of the basketball program in general as well). If a loose ball wandered away from a drill at one of the baskets, you would see a manager sprint across the floor like a Wimbledon ball boy hustling along the net at Centre Court. Our managers weren't just some guys who rolled the basketball racks onto the court and stood under the nets rebounding shots; they played major roles in our team practices and individual workouts. The coaching staff had the managers moving around in a choreographed manner. With the coming and going of each station rotation, managers would sprint to their next responsibility and position themselves to rebound, pass, play post defense with blocking pads, and more. Coach Knight had these workouts streamlined with as little downtime as possible. When there was a scheduled water break, Coach Knight didn't want the players wasting time going to and from the water coolers. So he had managers ready to sprint over to wherever the players on the court happened to be when the break time began. After a few squeezes from the water bottle you would hear, "Let's get back to work!" from Coach Knight, and in an instant everyone would go right back to the drill that had been on pause for the past sixty seconds.

Unfortunately, I knew I had to "get back to work" at the conclusion of most of my on-the-court workouts and off-the-court conditioning sessions during my freshman year, as I continued to struggle with each and every one. In one of my workouts I went up for a left-hand jump hook that was almost perfect, except that I missed it very short and to the left of the rim, which led to a quick Coach Knight evaluation that could have been heard in the rafters of Assembly Hall:

"There's that f_ _ _ ing weak shot again. If you want to play like a p_ _ _ s then go play [in the SEC]."

Needless to say, I had that feeling of needing to get back to work often after individual workouts with Coach Knight—as soon as the combined feeling of nausea and exhaustion had subsided.

I was making it through the individual workouts and the 6 AM weightlifting and conditioning sessions in a manner that would be classified more as surviving than thriving. Complicating the evaluation process even more for me was the fact that after all of our weightlifting and conditioning sessions each day, we would play pickup games against each other for about two hours. If I was having difficulties impressing the coaches in our individual workouts, then you can imagine how underwhelming my play was in these pickup games after I had already struggled through one or two hours of conditioning.

Pickup games (or "pickup scrimmages," as Coach Knight called them) had a very different meaning at IU from what I was accustomed. Even though Coach Knight wasn't allowed to direct our pickup games during this preseason time period according to NCAA rules, he still expected our play in these games to mirror the type of play he wanted to see on the court during practices and games. Thanks to old game films and the upperclassmen who ran our scrimmages, we ran the same offensive sets and played the same man-to-man defense in these pickup games that we would use versus a Big Ten opponent in the middle of the season. Any pickup game with a group of college basketball players is going to be competitive, but what made these games seem more important was that each of us was being graded by our managers, who were assigned to keep detailed individual stats of every pickup game.

When we finished playing for the day, managers would tally all the statistics and print up a stat sheet that would have each player's shooting percentages, along with the totals for offensive and defensive rebounds, assists, points, and turnovers. Then the managers would give copies to the coaching staff and leave a stack of copies in the middle of our locker room for the players (also, at the end of each week, there was a five-day total of all stats for each player). A lot of us treated these practice stat sheets as if they were graded exams from one of our courses, anxious to see if our studying had paid off in the form of a good evaluation. It was clear to me (and to everyone else, for that matter) that my stats in the first couple of weeks of our pickup scrimmages put me much closer to needing a tutor than to making the dean's list.

Another couple of weeks passed with workouts and pickup scrimmages, and it was now time for my first individual meeting with Coach Knight. I was down in the training room area when

I was told to head upstairs to the basketball offices, which were located just up the ramp from the main lobby of Assembly Hall, probably no more than a couple hundred yards above where I was standing in the training room. I quickly made my way up the stairs and up the ramp to the basketball offices where I was met with a welcoming greeting from Coach Knight's longtime secretary, Mary Ann Davis. She pointed me in the direction of an opened office door, through which I could hear a familiar booming voice as Coach Knight was in the middle of a friendly phone conversation.

I entered his spacious office and Coach Knight motioned me to have a seat in one of the two chairs in front of his desk. As he wrapped up his conversation, my eyes wandered around the packed room. Just behind me, there was a golf bag that was chock full of clubs. Leaning against the wall were also a variety of putters; it looked like he had been trying them out on the carpeted area in front of the couch, which was located at the back of the spacious office. I noticed on the wall next to his desk plaques of General Patton and President Lincoln, and prominently displayed on his desk was a baseball cap that simply read (in very bold letters across the front) "NCAA Sucks." Coach Knight hung up the phone and, as usual, skipped the pleasantries and got right to the point.

"Looking at the stat sheet, I see you made seventy-two shots this week in pickup scrimmages and that's not bad. You do have to improve on your turnovers and rebounding. I also see that you played in all seventeen games. That's good. A lot of freshmen come in and sit out a game here and there with injuries. Injuries that are injuries in high school aren't injuries here. The main thing is dedicating yourself to getting stronger. You do that and you're going to be a helluva player."

In the first semester of my first year as a college player, the pickup scrimmage stat sheets were one of the only ways to evaluate how I was stacking up versus D1 competition. Sure, I had shown some improvements from my first days in the weight room (back when I couldn't do a single pull-up in our preseason conditioning testing), in individual workouts and conditioning sessions (where my greatest accomplishment was not throwing up), and in our pickup games (where I was now getting dunked on with much less frequency—*woo-hoo*). But the truth was that in our intra-squad games, Andrae Patterson, Jason Collier, Robbie Eggers, Richard Mandeville, Charlie Miller, and Larry Richardson were all taking turns making me look like a player who was too weak and too soft to battle in the paint versus Big Ten caliber players. The daily beat-downs I experienced in our pickup games made me both *impressed* that my teammates could play at such a level after so much conditioning work, and *depressed* that I wasn't able to play near that same level with them yet.

Mr. Suit

It was my sophomore year and I had just finished a workout in the weight room and had about an hour and fifteen minutes to kill until practice. Instead of making a hurried trip back and forth to my apartment, I decided just to wait in the locker room and training room area for practice to start. As I was walking down the hallway from our locker room toward the training room to grab a protein shake, there was only one other person around in the entire downstairs complex, a gentleman in a nice-looking suit. He was leaning on the doorway of the training room with his back to me. As I got closer, I could see that he was using the training room phone that was on a shelf right next to the doorway. I had never seen this guy down here before, but I just figured that he was some IU administrator who had decided to pop in for a visit and use our phone. I stood behind the gentleman, waiting for him to allow me to pass through the training room entrance that he was currently obstructing. "Mr.

Knight Lines

Some guys don't know how to win;
others can't be defeated.

—Coach Knight
Freshman year, 10/1/97

Suit," however, was so into his chat that he had no idea anyone was around.

After a brief wait, my patience wore thin. Why is this suit down here using *our* phone and blocking *our* doorway, anyway? Didn't this guy have a phone in his own plush office that he could be using? Did he not know that one of the "big men" on campus, an Indiana Hoosier basketball player, was standing behind him waiting *and* becoming more and more parched by the second? Did Mr. Suit not know that a two-time (that's right, two whole times) Chevrolet Player of the Game was standing right behind him waiting to get in the training room?!! I finally had enough of this guy. I placed my hand on the side of his shoulder and in a nudging manner leveraged myself past him as I lobbed a sarcastic "excuse me" toward the mystery man. He momentarily broke from his telephone conversation just long enough to flash a big grin and whisper a friendly "how ya doin'" in my direction . . .

. . . and that's how I first met Isiah Thomas.

5

A Hall of Fame Kind of Day

It was pretty commonplace for former Hoosiers to return to Bloomington and pay a visit to Coach Knight and his current IU team. Players like Keith Smart, Alan Henderson, Calbert Cheaney, Landon Turner, Kent Benson, and others would come back and give of their time to impart some advice and encouragement. The talks and visits by all of these past players made one thing clear to us: when we put on an Indiana Hoosier uniform we were playing for much more than ourselves. We were playing for everyone who was in the Hoosier basketball family.

Our stalls in the Assembly Hall locker room had nameplates posted in them that announced which players from Hoosier history had used that same locker stall during their IU careers. The names in my locker were (Scott) May #42, (Steve) Risley #34, (Brian) Sloan #45, and (Damon) Bailey #22. It was more that enough to give us current players chills before heading out to same court where these legends were made, knowing that we occupied the same spot they had sat however many years before. It was one thing, of course, to become accustomed to having these names looking over our shoulders as we sat at our lockers. Now just imagine how it felt for us to see those very players walk into the locker room and stand in front of us. It gave us all a feeling of pride about our program's proud basketball past while also giving us a sense of responsibility about our program's future.

Being a part of the Hoosier basketball family led to many of these unforgettable interactions with past Hoosier greats, like the day Isiah Thomas came to talk to us. It's not every day that you get to look up from tying your basketball sneakers and see two men standing in front of you that have three NCAA championships and two NBA championships between them. Coach Knight had introduced a number of his past players to us, but the way he introduced Isiah had a different feel from the other introductions. Coach's intros for his former players were always done in a proud, albeit short and to-the-point manner. However, the way Coach introduced Isiah to us was more akin to the way a proud father introduces his son. After Coach introduced Isiah, he gave him the floor. Isiah didn't disappoint, and he didn't pull any punches that November day in 1999.

"Don't f_ _ _ in' embarrass us! You think you're playing hard, but you're not! You don't want to play against the guy who says, 'I'm going to be here for 40 f_ _ _ in' minutes!' Somebody has to step up and get some balls and say 'We're going to f_ _ _ in' go after you!' None of you here have won. Malone, Stockton, Barkley are all great, BUT they f_ _ _ in' lost all the time! It ain't f_ _ _ in' easy to win! Don't accept losing! Ninety-nine percent of the world has f_ _ _ in' lost! One percent of the world wins! There are people who talk [that] ain't won a f_ _ _ in' thing! Not at track, ping pong, pool. [Some guys] came in here and quit. Winners gravitate toward each other. Every f_ _ _ in' day I'd be eating steel if I was on a team ranked 40th in a poll!"

Coach gave Isiah a slap on the back in appreciation and told all of us to head out to the court and get warmed up for practice. Usually former players stayed around and watched us practice after they talked to the team. All of us hustled out to the court, eager for the opportunity to play in front of a college and NBA legend, anticipating that Isiah would also do as other past players had done, come out and sit courtside or in the stands and watch the day's practice. However, the hope that Isiah was coming out to watch us was thwarted about fifteen minutes into practice when we all realized at the same time that he wasn't going to be coming out to watch us play after all. But we didn't feel disappointment. We actually were feeling the exact opposite.

Knight Lines

Champions don't have buddies who f_ _ k things up! When I talk about champions, you'd better listen!

—Coach Knight

Junior year, 11/28/99

This was because as we heard the doors of the gym open, we turned to see the leader of the Pistons' Bad Boys himself walking right toward us, wearing a red and white no. 11 practice jersey and shorts. Just minutes removed from his speech to us about defense and competing, he now appeared ready to back up those locker room words with action on the court. Mr. Thomas had no intention of spending his time in Assembly Hall watching *us* play the game of basketball. To the contrary, Isiah had every intention of us watching *him* play the game of basketball.

I had to shake the cobwebs out of my head as Coach Knight and his assistants set up the two teams for the scrimmage that was getting ready to begin. What basketball player, much less a Hoosier basketball player, wouldn't dream of this chance to be on the court with a man that had the hardware, rings, and reputation that Isiah Thomas had? It's not every day that you have a chance to be on the court with a player who in his career had stood toe-to-toe with the likes of Bird, Magic, and MJ and gave those legends all they could handle and more. All that being said, though, I have to be honest, as we were getting set to start our scrimmage the thought that was on my mind was this: "What can this old, little guy still *really* do on a basketball court?"

Coach Knight set the teams. Now it was time to find out what this old NBA Top 50 player of all time was still made of. "It couldn't be all that much," I thought to myself. It didn't take long to realize that this line of thinking was a far cry from the truth. Our fantasy basketball camp quickly turned into a basketball boot camp. If someone had been at practice that day who had never watched a college or professional basketball game, they would have noticed within the first five minutes that there was something exceptional about the player wearing the no. 11 jersey (no, Dane Fife, I am not referring to you). Some people are put on this earth to do certain things. There are some who can learn to play a note on a musical instrument almost as easily as they learn to breathe. There are some who are so blessed with artistic abilities that they can fill a canvas with exactly what they are imagining in their mind's eye. And then there are those who were meant solely to perform their artistry on a basketball court, apparently no matter their age.

This practice and this moment couldn't have meant any more to anyone else on our team than it did to our senior guard, A. J. Guyton. Our future first-team All-American and Big Ten Player of the Year had more than a few basketball connections to Isiah. A. J. hailed from Peoria, Illinois, just a couple of hours from the Chicago courts where Isiah grew up playing. A. J. was a shooting guard with point guard handles, and Isiah was a point guard with a shooting guard's touch. Their size and playing style had quite a few similarities too, especially when it came to the cross-over moves they both wielded like weapons on the basketball court. A. J. even chose to wear no. 11 while he was in the NBA playing for the Chicago Bulls. It was something special that day to have a chance to see a legendary Hoosier guard come back to the very gym that began his legendary career and challenge the current Hoosier star guard. A. J. and Isiah were the show as the red and white teams battled that day. I quickly realized during this particular scrimmage that my first, second, and third priorities were to screen for A. J., and that my fourth priority was to rebound, and then promptly kick it back out to A. J.

Coach Knight rarely had a running clock on the scoreboard for our scrimmages. Like a conductor of a symphony, he would guide us through the ebbs and flows of our scrimmage until the team had gotten into a good groove, and then he would usually wait for one last solid play before he ended practice on a good note. Several minutes into our scrimmage that day, practice came to a close on a play that none of the players, coaches, managers, or trainers will ever forget. Coach Knight's players generally develop a pretty good sense for when he is going to wrap up practice and send us all back to the locker room. I think A. J. and Isiah both figured that we were coming down to the last possession or two of practice, so they decided to set the stage for one more showdown on the Assembly Hall floor. A. J. waved off any screeners who might have dared think of coming into the picture as he and Mr. 11 set the scene. A. J. had the ball a few feet behind the three-point line at the top of the key with only Isiah standing between him and what was almost certainly going to be the final possession of the day. A. J. was determined to make this already memorable day perfect by ending practice and his personal battle against a basketball icon with a successful one-on-one move. A. J. made his move. He took his live dribble left and set up for a smooth crossover back to his right. A. J.'s arms and hands worked in perfect sync with his feet as he maneuvered his body past Isiah. But the ball didn't go with him.

In a flash of quickness that you would have thought was long ago left behind in the Palace of Auburn Hills, Isiah cleanly relieved A. J. of his dribble by popping the ball loose into the backcourt near the state of Indiana logo at center court. A. J., one of the quickest and best players in the Big Ten at the time, reacted immediately and turned to recover the loose ball, which was now behind him, but still well within reach of his lengthy wingspan. A. J.'s hands were milliseconds from recovering the loose ball, but his window of opportunity shut as a thirty-eight-year-old, twelve-time NBA All-Star and former NBA Finals MVP dove to the floor and smothered the ball, clutching it with both arms into his chest.

Coach Knight stopped practice, and it was a good thing he did, too, because everyone in the gym was stunned to the point of being frozen in their tracks. We were all just standing there, coaches and managers included, silently taking in as cool a moment as we had ever seen on a basketball court. The truly great competitors don't wait to "pick their spots," "turn it on when they need to," or "flip a switch," depending on the moment. The truly great demand it of themselves to have that switch flipped on at all times. What a perfect example this play was for a group of young college players needing a lesson on what it was to consistently compete. Here was a man who had absolutely nothing more to prove on a basketball court, putting forth maximum effort simply because he demanded that level of effort from himself every time he set foot on the floor.

As Isiah stood up, Coach Knight told all of us to head to the locker room and shower. Coach walked toward his 1981 NCAA championship point guard. The two basketball Hall of Famers walked off the Assembly Hall court together. As it turns out, we were all watching the last time the two greatest Hoosier basketball legends would ever be on the Assembly Hall court together at once. A proud Coach Knight walked off the court with his arm draped around his point guard's slender shoulders. In his hands, Isiah was still carrying that loose ball.

Gilligan versus the Skipper

Not surprisingly, considering their fiery personalities, Mike Lewis and Dane Fife once got into an angry exchange after practice one day. When it reached its tipping point they rushed at each other, both of them with intentions to brawl. Luke Recker was able to reach Fife in time to hold him back from getting to Lewis, but no one stepped in to hold back Lewis—so he got to Fife and delivered one good shot to Fife's face, which left him with a scar on his lip. Coach Knight's response was to leave boxing gloves in their lockers the next day. Even though college moments like this one are all water under the bridge to the combatants today (Fife and Lewis have since taken their arguments from the basketball court to the greens and fairway), Fife recently summed up the episode by simply stating, "F_ _ _ ing Lewis."

During my second season of playing basketball for the Hoosiers, I found myself in a not-so-physical discussion that had more to do with life jackets than boxing gloves. A couple of family friends from back home in Tennessee, Dave Rhodes (our school system's superintendent at the time) and David Young (owner of a funeral home in Perry County), came with my granddad to Bloomington for a game that (luckily for them) we won. That being the case, Coach Knight was in a pretty good mood and asked my granddad, Dave, and David about how the hunting and fishing was back home in Tennessee. They told him that he should come down for a hunting or fishing trip sometime.

Knight Lines

I've only shot three players since I've been here [at IU], only three. But . . . it only took three shots. So when I walk in here with a shotgun you just had better watch out.

—Coach Knight

Freshman year, 11/1997

When I first heard about this conversation I thought, "There's no way that trip ever happens." A guy like Coach Knight, who travels all over the world on hunting and fishing expeditions, isn't going to go down to "Podunk Tennessee" (as he affectionately called my hometown) to hunt or fish. Well, just a few months later I was proven wrong when my granddad called me one April afternoon in between classes of my spring semester to inform me that Coach Knight and his son Pat were heading for Lobelville for a post-basketball season fishing trip. Their trip included three boats that day. Dave and his father-in-law, Joe Sweeney, were in the last boat, David and Pat Knight were in the middle boat, and resident fishing, golfing, and coon hunting expert Bob Turnbow was with Coach Knight in the lead boat. It was several hours before I heard back from my granddad. I knew they were going out for more than a "three-hour tour," but I didn't think it would take this long to get an update. I was eager to hear how Coach Knight's maiden voyage on the Buffalo River had gone. I knew my pals back home on the fishing trip with Coach Knight had to be pinching themselves, cruising down the banks of the Buffalo River with the coaching legend they had all been fans of years before I had ever thought about playing at Indiana. All I knew about the fishing trip was that my granddad was dropping off Coach Knight and Pat at the boats in the northern part of Perry County at the Flatwoods bridge, and then he was to pick them up a few hours later down river in Linden and take them to my home in Lobelville, where they would grill steaks for supper. Later that evening, I finally received a call from Granddad and learned some of the details of the Knights' Perry County fishing trip. Granddad told me that everything at the drop-off point had gone smoothly, but that he knew something had gone awry when he picked them up later that day and noticed Coach Knight ringing out his socks on the river bank.

One of the persons on the fishing trip, David Young, filled me in later on exactly what had happened in an area of the Buffalo River known as Rockhouse, just north of the community where my granddad grew up, known as Flatwoods. As Bob Turnbow drove his boat between the banks of the Buffalo River toward the next fishing hole, he and Coach Knight were enjoying a nice chat. However, the combination of noise from the boat motor and the wind had made it difficult for Coach Knight to hear what Mr. Turnbow was saying, so he got up to move closer to the front. Unfortunately for Coach Knight, he wasn't aware that a bend in the river was fast approaching and that he had chosen a most inopportune time to lean up out of his seat. So right then and there in the middle of Perry County, Tennessee, my friend Bob accidently threw my Coach Bob overboard into the rock-bottom waters of the Buffalo River.

David and Pat were in the boat behind Coach Knight, and as he and Pat made the turn around the river bend, Pat didn't have much sympathy for his dad. He let out a good laugh as they passed Coach Knight, who was now swimming toward his St. Louis Cardinals cap that was floating away from him (Pat told David that they had to retrieve the hat since Coach Knight's longtime friend, Tony LaRussa, had just given it to him while he was visiting spring training a week earlier). Overall, Coach Knight took the whole ordeal really well and was incredibly kind to his Perry County tour guides. While they were eating rib-eye steaks that night at my house (Coach Knight told them to cook his steak for "two minutes on each side"), David Young told me something that Coach Knight shared with them while they were all sitting at my kitchen table after supper. Coach said, "*I'll tell you guys this, if I can get Kirk's a_ s to play defense, I'll make him into an All-American.*"

Fast-forward about four months later into the start of my junior year of playing basketball. It was October 25, 2000—Coach Knight's birthday. It was a Hoosier basketball team tradition to take a cake out to the gym floor for Coach Knight right after our practice had ended. I don't know how long this tradition had been going on, but for the years I was there the process went like clockwork. Coach Knight would end practice, all the players would go to the locker room and pick up the birthday cake that the long-time head trainer, Tim Garl, had ordered. The team would line up and walk the cake out to Coach Knight and sing a short rendition of "Happy Birthday." Shortly thereafter, Coach Knight would come back into the locker room and say a quick "thank you" to us for the cake before we all headed to our respective destinations for the evening. That year for some reason, I had gotten it into my head that I was going to change the routine a little bit and add something to the birthday celebration. Unfortunately, this turned out to be in the form of a moronic comment. I had the intention of presenting an actual gift to go along with my comment, but I couldn't find what I wanted and just decided to go with a quick birthday "zinger" directed at

Coach Knight instead. As Coach finished his quick "thank you" and headed toward the door, I began the line that I had been practicing in my mind for the past five minutes. I cleared my throat and said, "After that fishing trip you had back in Tennessee, I thought about getting you a life jacket for your birthday."

I had just enough cowardice to not speak up while Coach Knight was standing right in front of me, and yet I had just enough bravery to say the line loud enough for him to hear it, even though I thought he was probably already out of earshot. About fifteen whole seconds passed after I said my little joke. I sat there in my chair in front of my locker stall and looked around at my teammates with a grin, brimming with confidence after showing everyone that I had the guts to take a little good-humored shot at The General himself. Then all that confidence left my body faster than a Miami Heat fan leaves a home game. Coach Knight came barreling around the corner of the locker room entrance with a nimbleness I didn't know he was capable of and stood ten inches away from the tips of my red and white Converse sneakers. His finger was about that same distance from the tip of my nose when he took a breath and sharply said,

> *If your friends knew how to drive a f_ _ _ ing boat*
> *I wouldn't need a f_ _ _ ing life jacket!*

As Coach eased back from his position in front of me, he shot a slight smirk my way as he turned away. I was really glad that we had just had a good practice, I was really glad that Coach was in a joking mood, and I was really, *really* glad that I had not found an actual life jacket to give to Coach Knight because he might have made me put it to use while chucking me into the waters of nearby Lake Monroe.

6

Talking about Practice

"I bet you only have one stoplight in your hometown!" If you're from a small town then you've probably heard jokes like this one as often as I have (to be exact, though, my hometown has *zero* stoplights). I know a lot of jokes can be and are made at the expense of folks from small towns, and that just comes with the territory when you're from a place where people give directions by using the names of creeks rather than roads (like Cane Creek, Cypress Creek, Crooked Creek, Cedar Creek—and that's just the ones in my county that start with the letter "C"!). But there is one thing for which not too many small-town country folks get made fun of, and that's their willingness to put in a hard day's work.

I may have grown up in a town that was an hour away from the nearest Target and O'Charley's, but every day I was around people with amazing work ethics. My mom and granddad were great examples of this. Even the kids I grew up with were incredibly hard workers at young ages, and many of them worked jobs year round. Some of my best friends in elementary and middle school all put in hours and hours of work at saw mills, farms, family businesses, and other places, doing work that would make most grown men complain. I always admired my friends who were constantly putting in a hard day's work, sometimes right after school. I myself never had any kind of regular, paying job growing up. Of course I did have the normal chores around the house like taking out the trash, trimming the hedges, and mowing the lawn, but my family's "family business" was teaching and coaching. I ended up learning about the importance of work a little bit differently from a lot of my friends. My mom and granddad took a different approach to teach me lessons on work ethic. They taught me about work ethic by letting me log hours of work in the gym to develop my basketball skills. The lessons I learned from them back then are still paying dividends to this day.

While I was growing up, my mom told me on several occasions, "Son, as long as you're putting in time working at the gym, I'm not going to ask you to work at a job." A single mom on a teacher's salary could have definitely benefited from her son

Knight Lines

This is not Tennessee Central! Do we still have any of those diapers around? Some of those rubber diapers for our Tennessee boy?

—Coach Knight

Freshman year, 1/26/98, at a practice in which Coach felt that my play had been somewhat below Big Ten standards but just right for fictitious Tennessee Central University

having a job after school or during the summer to help make ends meet. Much like the way Coach Knight would see something in me as a player during my freshman year that I didn't know was there, my mom believed in me enough to allow me to focus my time and energy toward pursuing my dream of playing college basketball someday. From the outside looking in, many probably thought that my mom was being way too optimistic when it came to her bullish expectations for her tall son. Yes, I was a 6'2" seventh grader, but I was a 6'2" seventh grader who couldn't touch the bottom of the backboard. That being said, Mom believed I could work my way into a scholarship, although I do remember her tempering her expectations at one point by saying that even a "partial scholarship" would be a great achievement (she probably said that the day she saw her 6'4" eighth grade son "jump" as high he could and barely touch the net). I realize now how fortunate I was to have a mom who would give her son this kind of opportunity. I also realize just how fortunate I was to have my granddad there to teach me how to approach this opportunity.

The key to Granddad's approach to sports was simple: "*Work at making your work fun.*"

He was a master at making anything into some sort of fun, competitive game. If we had a deck of cards that was incomplete—no problem, he would get an empty trash can and turn the useless deck of cards into a "Who Can Make the Most Cards into the Trash Can World Series." I'll never forget when I was ten years old and he and I were sitting outside a mall in a park area during a Nashville shopping trip Mom and Granny wanted to take. We were just sitting on a park bench killing time waiting for Mom and Granny to come back from the stores when basically out of thin air (actually, it was out of Granny's shopping bag she had left with us) Granddad created a homerun derby for me out of a stick and a "ball" that he had made from wadding up scrap paper into a recently emptied, egg-shaped pantyhose

Knight Lines

Practice is your lottery ticket. A lot of people want to win the lottery and they have a 1 in 10,000,000 chance to have their ticket drawn. You guys have been given your f_ _ _ ing lottery ticket in the scholarship you've been given to come here! Of the 29,996 students, you 14 guys have the greatest chance of winning the lottery. You have the winning lottery ticket, all you have to do is cash it in by practicing and working hard.

—Coach Knight

Freshman year, 10/1997

container. When Granny got back she wasn't as thrilled with our new "baseball" as we were, especially when she found her newly purchased pantyhose loose in her shopping bag! Granddad taught me how to improve at basketball by making my practice time so fun and competitive that I wasn't even aware of the amount of work I was doing or the benefits I was receiving. As a kid I was allowed to compete with my mind focused solely on the moment I was in. I didn't have to devote a single thought toward any consequences of failure from my granddad or mom. Granddad still placed a high level of importance on winning, but he did so with an emphasis on the importance of the approach to the game and not the result. Results can be random, cruel, and often completely out of our control. However, what is never out of our control is the approach we take as we practice toward our goals and play through our failures.

Speaking of failures. . .

I definitely had a disappointing NBA career—and I do realize that I'm using the word *career* here very, very loosely. I never thought I would be an NBA all-star, but going into my rookie season I felt certain that I could carve out a career of being a consistent 20 minutes per game rotation guy that could give a team a solid 8 points, 8 rebounds, and 6 fouls a night. However, I failed miserably to live up to even these expectations. I wanted to get my rookie year off to a great start, but I struggled with my shooting in the preseason with the Charlotte Hornets and that seemed to seal my fate as far as head coach Paul Silas was concerned. Before our first regular-season game, the Hornets traded one of their centers (and longtime NBA malcontent) Derrick Coleman for Robert Traylor, George Lynch, and Jerome Moiso, who all played the same forward position as me. Adding these guys to the two other outstanding forwards we already had on the team, Jamal Mashburn and P. J. Brown, meant that there was going to be a logjam of forwards on the Hornets' roster.

If I had played better in my rookie preseason, perhaps I would have gotten more of an opportunity in the regular season, but Silas didn't seem very interested in developing young talent as long as he could plug an NBA veteran into his lineup. That preseason is one of my greatest choke jobs that I've had to learn to live with. It also didn't help that I had the same problem that many rookies run into: getting drafted by a good team vying for a playoff berth. The fact of the matter is there are many more opportunities for young NBA players to play significant minutes on teams that are out of the playoff chase by midseason or soon thereafter. I hadn't put an enormous amount of stock into my disappointing preseason play, because I thought that there would be plenty of time to earn minutes by playing well in practices over the course of the lengthy seven-month season. After all, performing well in practices was the way I had always earned playing time everywhere else. I soon found out that was not going to be the case in the NBA.

It would have been nice if Silas had given me a little more of an opportunity to become a contributing player for the team that drafted me with the sixteenth overall pick. But in my first two NBA seasons Silas played me in consecutive games only *nine* times, and he never played me double-digit minutes in consecutive games (the closest I ever got my first year was logging 12 minutes versus the Lakers, followed by a game against the Jazz where I played 5 minutes). My second season was even more miserable than my rookie season in this regard. In that second season the longest that Silas played me in a game was 8 minutes, and the most minutes he ever played me that year in consecutive games was eleven (8 minutes versus the Wizards and then 3 minutes versus the Grizzlies the next game). It was a depressing shock to my system to see just how marginalized the importance of practice was in the NBA compared to that of college. I was used to practice always being the key avenue for a player to earn playing opportunities. In all honesty, knowing what I know now about NBA practices, no one should really have an issue with this famous Allen Iverson quote: "I mean, listen, we're sitting here talking about practice, not a game, not a game, not a game, but we're talking about practice." He was being dismissive of the importance of NBA practices, and that line of thinking is pretty spot-on from what I experienced. However, Iverson's take couldn't be more different from the experience of playing basketball at Indiana for Coach Knight. It was an absolute, cold, hard fact that if you were going to be a successful college basketball player under Coach Knight, you better believe there was going to be a lot of talk about practice—and a ton of work in those practices. Coach Knight's practices required a player to be prepared for a three-part test. The parts of this test included knowing *what* to do, *when* to do it, and *how* to do it. *What* are you going to do if a defender overplays the passing lane? *When* are you going to use a pass fake against a zone defense? *How* do you prepare yourself to be ready to make the correct play? The only way that you can get high grades in a course is by being prepared and doing the necessary work *before* you ever walk into the classroom, or into the gymnasium, as the case may be.

Knight Lines

This is not a practice, it's a preparation.

—Coach Knight

Freshman year, 10/1/97

Granddad's "work at making your work fun" approach was worth its weight in gold as I applied it toward playing for Coach Knight. It was because of my granddad that I never saw competition as something to be dreaded or feared. If I had grown up with my family constantly pushing and critiquing me every step of the way as I pursued my basketball dreams, I believe that would have been the worst possible way to prepare for playing for Coach Knight. It may seem the opposite of that would be true. However, the way Granddad instilled in me how important it was to work at making my work fun, no matter how tough and pressure-filled the work may be, was a perfect foundation to build on as I worked to meet the high standards of Coach Knight.

In 2010, two years since I had last talked to him, Coach Knight unexpectedly called me right after the end of Super Bowl XLIV between the New Orleans Saints and the Indianapolis

Knight Lines

It would be a lot to ask of you guys to be able to beat a good team after just two practices— but not by the third!

—Coach Knight

Junior year, 10/16/99

Colts. Even though in that game Saints' quarterback Drew Brees was named Super Bowl MVP, going 32 for 39 for 288 yards, two touchdowns, and no interceptions, it was someone else that caught Coach Knight's eye that night, and he was calling me out of the blue just to point that out. Upon answering the phone, the first sentence I heard from Coach Knight wasn't about Brees, but a former Indiana University cornerback named Tracy Porter. Coach Knight (as usual) began talking on the phone like we were already in the middle of a conversation: *"That kid did his job the whole game with nothing to show for it, but he kept putting himself into the right position to make a play every possession until it paid off with a play that won the game."* Porter (who played at IU from 2004 to 2007) had picked off a Peyton Manning pass near the end of the fourth quarter and ran it back 74 yards for a touchdown, giving the Saints a 31–17 lead and their final margin of victory. It was no surprise at all that Coach Knight would attach himself to a great defensive play by an Indiana Hoosier. I think at this juncture that's just a permanent part of his DNA. And it was also no surprise that even all these years after I had last played for him, Coach was still trying to get across the point to me what good defense by a Hoosier looked like. Porter's play was the kind that Coach Knight loved. It was a play that took awareness, it was a play that eliminated any hope of victory for the opposing team, and it was a play that happened as a result of a player's preparation for the situation.

If you were going to be a successful basketball player for Coach Knight, it would begin (or end) for you in his practices. Players can only move closer to realizing their potential if they make a commitment and dedicate themselves to preparation. Practice was the ultimate litmus test for Coach Knight to see if a player was truly buying into the rules and systems that he was teaching. So what did it mean to be prepared to practice for Coach Knight? Let's just say that you didn't want to be a guy in practice who was consistently setting screens two seconds too soon and getting into your help-side defensive position two seconds too late. If that was the case, then you might as well have told your family back home that the next time they tune in to ESPN to watch you play, they would be better off just watching the movie *Hoosiers,* because they would have as good a chance seeing you play for Coach Norman Dale's Hickory High team as they would seeing you play for Coach Knight's Indiana Hoosiers.

It's easy as a player to allow practices to become an unfortunate necessity that you want to see come and go as quickly as possible just so you can get to the next game on the schedule. I

Knight Lines

This is not a d _ _ n game, it's a crusade!

—Coach Knight

Junior year, 2/12/00

think all players get lulled into this way of thinking from time to time. I think that I had fallen into this trap along the way during my senior year in high school. I didn't dread practice, but practices had just become something to do between games, which is absolutely the wrong way to approach the game of basketball. An accidental yet valuable by-product of the redshirt experience was that I learned to *love* practice. I stopped looking at my redshirt freshman year as a season that had zero games, and instead began to approach it with the mindset that I had 100 games on my schedule.

Our practices became everything to me that season. Practices were my only competitive outlet (besides some golf I played on the side with Tom Geyer and manager Brandon Sorrell). Even though there were no fans in the stands or TV cameras broadcasting, it was my own personal CBS Game of the Week every time the ball rack was rolled out onto the Assembly Hall court for practice. Since practices became my games, this meant I had to make out my own personal practice schedule in order to be properly prepared for my own personal game schedule. I scheduled managers to come in during the mornings or early afternoons so I could get some shooting done between classes, and I used the on-campus student recreation center's basketball courts on some of our rare off-days. I had never before worked this hard *preparing* myself for practices. Coach Knight made me realize that taking one step back in the preparation process and targeting each practice as a game could lead to exponential improvement.

Basketball players from small schools can make for easy targets when it comes to critiquing their college potential. I remember one national recruiting magazine describing me before my senior year as a "big fish in a little pond that is a mid-major talent" (a clipping that I taped to my bedroom mirror for several years). One of the reasons I desperately didn't want to be redshirted was because I didn't want those who thought I had overshot my talent level by signing with Indiana to feel any kind of validation. The fear of being redshirted had motivated me enough that I did much better than I expected in the last couple of weeks of workouts leading up to our first official team practice, Midnight Madness. Because of this I still held onto a sliver of hope that if I had a good practice and played well in the traditional Red–White Midnight Madness scrimmage that I might actually earn the right to wear the candy-striped warm-up pants, get my own no. 35 Hoosiers jersey, and dodge being redshirted my freshman season (which was the rumor I was beginning to hear around Assembly Hall).

A lot of schools' Midnight Madness practices are just a show for the fans. But my first Midnight Madness practice with Coach Knight at the helm was very much like the other 300-plus practices with him. OK, aside from the fact we had around 9,000 fans at this particular practice, it was just like any other practice. No dunk contests, no three-point contests, and no Dickie V setting up half-court shots by fans from the stands for prizes. Coach had waited about six months for the next day of team practice to arrive from the end of the previous season and now that it was finally here, he had no intention of wasting a minute of it on frivolous fan indulgences. Coach Knight's focus in practice is as legendary as his career record. I don't know what his eyesight was officially, but his players felt that the nearly sixty-year-old coach had 20/10 vision. This was especially true at Midnight Madness, the first time that our team was on public display on the basketball court. It was remarkable how Coach Knight could be teaching a player about proper post defense technique on one end of the court and out of the corner of his eye spot me ninety feet away miss a box-out in a two-on-two drill and yell in my direction,

"D_ _ _ it HASTON! If you're going to play that soft then go ahead and turn your jersey over and just play for the other f_ _ _ ing team!"

Knight Lines

There are two types of players, ones that let things happen [and ones] that make things happen.

—Coach Knight

Sophomore year, 12/5/98

My play was average at best during the Midnight Madness practice and the intrasquad scrimmage. I made some shots and my block-outs and rebounding were pretty solid. But it seemed all night long I was constantly having one good possession followed by two bad possessions. One of the main offensive rules that Coach Knight preached at us constantly was to "keep good spacing." In order for our motion offense to work as effectively and efficiently as he wanted, all five players on the floor needed to keep good spacing from each other in order to properly set up cuts, set screens, and make good passes. My spacing that first scrimmage was far from ideal in Coach Knight's well-trained eyes, as evidenced by this comment barked in my direction: *"Having two guys that closely spaced is like trying to fit two pints of s_ _ t into a one-pint container!"* Ahead of our Midnight Madness practice Coach Knight wrote these five keys to being great on the whiteboard in our locker room:

1. CONCENTRATION
2. AWARENESS
3. RECOGNITION
4. REACTION
5. EXECUTION

After our first practice was over I felt like *maybe* I had gotten a passing grade on one of these five keys. As the deadline to red-shirt quickly approached, I hoped that I could still show enough improvement in the next practice to earn a roster spot.

My main mistake going into my first season as an Indiana Hoosier was thinking that the work ethic I had had in high school which had gotten me a D1 scholarship would lead me to similar success as a college player. In high school, basketball is a game. In the Big Ten, basketball is a job. Don't get me wrong. I'm not stating that as a complaint because it was a great job to have. I'm just saying that if you are playing a Division I college sport,

Knight Lines

Calbert Cheaney was the best practice player. He was the first on the court and last one to leave.

—Coach Knight

Sophomore year, 3/4/99

then the amount of time a player spends doing "student work" doesn't come close to the amount of time a player spends doing "athlete work." There may not be a paycheck at the end of the week, but when you are clocking 50–70 hours a week of lifting, practicing, film watching, traveling, and then playing in games, athletes are definitely putting in job-like hours. (By the way, I don't think I'm going too far out on a limb here to say that there aren't many major D1 basketball or football programs in the country that actually adhere to the outdated twenty-hour max rule the NCAA still has on its books.) A strong "high school work ethic" can get you into the door of a college arena. However, if you aren't willing to put in the effort and the time to keep up to the pace of the competitive environment around you, then not too many doors will open for you during your college sports career.

I definitely had to relearn what it meant to have a strong work ethic on the basketball court in my first season at Indiana. Consistently shooting a hundred extra shots and doing some extra plyometric box jumps after practices may separate you from your competition in high school hoops, but if you want to excel in the world of D1 college basketball, then you need to get used to calling that type of extra work something else—a warm-up.

11/5/97: Three Weeks into Team Practices My Freshman Year

Coach Knight told me near the end of practice that he wanted me to stay behind after he dismissed the team to the locker room so he could talk with me for a few minutes. As practice ended and the court cleared, I made my way down to where Coach Knight was sitting, which was his favorite seat in Assembly Hall, on the large red safety padding underneath one of the main basketball goal stanchions. I walked over and sat next to him. As Coach began to talk, I looked around and noticed we were the only two people in the entire gym.

"You know how to play basketball as well as any freshman I've had here."

This was nice to hear, but I could feel the "but" coming at this point.

"But the fact is, with Charlie [Miller], [Richard] Mandeville, [Robbie] Eggers, and [Andrae] Patterson all here right now, they can fill the forward and center positions. Then next year they're all

gone and then you're there. You're going to be a regular here and more than that for four years. And by redshirting, you can improve on your strength and stamina. Sometimes me and [assistant coach Norm] Ellenberger will chuckle during practice after you do something—a tip-in or a pass. You can do things that some bigs just can't do. You see the floor. You just know the game."

I knew Coach was letting me down as gently as possible because he knew how badly I wanted to make the roster my freshmen year. One of the things a lot of the upperclassmen told the underclassmen was that Coach Knight knew how to play all of his players, and one way to do that was by holding talented freshmen in reserve as redshirts. Then, as the seasons passed and your play improved, so would the expectations—and with these expectations came a much more difficult grading scale. It wasn't a surprise to go from a "great" freshman who never played to a starter who could receive this type of assessment: *"You're the big, dumb son of a b_ _ _ h that we brought in from Tennessee to rebound, not to shoot 20-foot jump shots."* So I learned to take Coach Knight's kind words with a grain of salt, but I also knew by this point that Coach Knight wasn't one to pass around compliments unless there was some meaning behind them.

I have heard my granddad say from the pulpit a number of times, "Heaven is a prepared place for a prepared people." It didn't take long to learn that an Indiana Hoosiers practice was a prepared place for a prepared player. One of the points that Coach Knight got across early on was that players should be more concerned with preparing to play the game rather than preparing to play the opponents. Coach Knight taught me that every minute I wasted on being disappointed about being red-shirted was time that could be used to prepare myself for the next practice and the next basketball season. Another point that he got across to me my freshman year was that players don't reach their potential by the work they do in team practices. Too many players get trapped into thinking that team practices alone are the launching point in preparing themselves for playing in games. There is only a certain amount of time that a coach can devote to individual skill development during team practices because of all the other team preparations that must be done. It's the individual preparation before and after team practices where players separate themselves from their competition. If you're banking on becoming a great player based solely on what you do in a team practice, then you're fooling yourself. Preparation is a great equalizer. A player with good talent who is dedicated to preparation can gain ground on, and even pass, an unprepared player blessed with great talent. Both your game and your goals have to evolve or your competition will pass you by eventually. If a player was bringing potential and not preparation to Coach Knight's practice every day, then that player wasn't going to be given much of a chance come game time. Coach Knight didn't stay impressed with a player's potential for very long. You would never hear Coach Knight say, "Well, that kid isn't very much of a practice player, but I think he'll be good when the game starts."

When I was a freshman, Coach Knight seemed to have a much more optimistic view of my college basketball career than one of his assistant coaches had. I overheard a comment that "Kirk is not a player that's going to be able to play at the Big Ten level," which may not provide much encouragement, but it

Knight Lines

I don't get on your a _ s unless you are worth it!

—Coach Knight

Sophomore year, 1/29/99

can supply plenty of motivation. Coach Knight saw a potential in me that almost everyone else had missed, including myself (and one of his own assistants). He saw the future player inside of me long before I even felt it. That one-on-one talk Coach had with me about redshirting still means a lot to me today, but it meant even more to that skinny, struggling freshman in 1997. Learning of someone else's belief in you can impact your level of motivation and confidence in a way that can't be fully appreciated unless you have experienced it. I was fortunate that Coach Knight was there to positively impact my life with his belief in me. And that's why it's so important for all of us to search for the capabilities that may be hiding within those around us. It's scary to think how much potential is out there waiting to be unlocked by just a few encouraging words.

Can You Hear Me Now?

Early in our 1999–2000 season, when I was a redshirt sophomore, we had an embarrassing home loss in our very own Indiana Classic, losing to Indiana State 63–60. That was our first loss of the season, making us at the time 6–1. The following practice Coach Knight told us, "*Losing is unacceptable to me. We took 7 shots off the dribble because we didn't have good set-ups on offense. We didn't care about winning! There's a pride that has to accompany skill and what I saw Saturday night was selfish. Most people don't have a chance to do something memorable. We've beaten seven teams [this season], six other teams and ourselves.*" It was the most upset I had seen Coach Knight that season, at least until February.

It was then that we had a late-game collapse and lost at Minnesota 77–75, despite having led most of the game. One of the reasons for the late collapse was the soft defense I played at the

Knight Lines

The mistakes you DON'T make win games.

—Coach Knight

Sophomore year, 1998–99

end while guarding Minnesota's star center, Joel Przybilla. Coach had some choice words of wisdom at our next practice, for both me and A. J.: "*Guyton and Haston, you two had 51 points combined last night, but if I factor in you two's defense it was a net 15 points.*" Coach moved on to talk about the shot I took late in the game that wasn't quite up to his standards: "[*That was*] *one of the greatest p_ _ _ y shots of all time with the game on the line.*"

We were now 7–3 in Big Ten conference play, and at that point I was averaging 18 points and 10 rebounds in conference games. But none of this mattered at all to Coach Knight as long as I was having significant defensive lapses on the basketball court and in practice. Coach wasn't one to shy away from giving you an honest, straightforward assessment of your play, and if you for some reason didn't want to listen and pay attention to what he was telling you, well, then, he also had some advice for just such an occasion: "*Go [ahead], go somewhere in the country and be coached by someone who won't get on your a-s!*"

Three days removed from our ugly loss at Minnesota, Coach Knight was still seething about what he called my "*soft-a-s defense.*" Our next game was against Michigan. My teammates and I were in the locker room waiting for Coach Knight to come in for his post-practice debriefing, after what I felt had been a pretty good practice for us. Coach Knight calmly walked in and began to boldly write what looked like a phone number on the white board, and then he said:

> *Kirk, please give [an out-of-conference coach] a call.*
> *His number is 1-800-IMA-P_ _ S. If you want to play*
> *soft, then call this number. I'm sure he will take you*
> *there. Maybe you and him can play checkers together.*

And with that, our post-practice debriefing was over. Coach Knight and his assistants exited the locker room, leaving our trainer Tim Garl behind to give us our instructions on when we would be heading out for Ann Arbor. But before he even opened his mouth, he saw the phone number on the board, then looked over at me and grinned.

We flew into Ann Arbor later that evening and settled into our hotel at around 5:30 PM. We had a very consistent schedule on our road trips. After arriving at the hotel, the players and managers would usually eat supper at the hotel's restaurant while the coaching staff went to a restaurant that Coach Knight had selected. After we finished with our supper, the players would then go up to Coach Knight's suite, where the managers had the projector and projection screen set up to watch game film of our opponent. Coach Knight always wanted the players to have a film session without any coaches present, and he let the upper-classmen take the lead in going over the game plan and scouting report that Coach Knight had been going over in the practices leading up to the game. After that, we would all go back to our rooms and kill some time until one last film session and team meeting around 9 PM with Coach Knight and the coaching staff in his room.

We all took a seat in the room and got set for Coach Knight to go over the Michigan game film again. But before he started the film, he had something he needed to get off of his chest:

Coach: *Kirk, [the 1-800-IMA-P_ _ S college coach]*
called again tonight. What should I tell him?

Me: Tell him I'm going to be busy the next two
years.

Coach (cuts me a look out of the corner of his eyes
and shoots a crooked smile in my direction):
Well . . . that depends on how well you rebound.

After Coach analyzed more of the game film and instructed
us on what actions their offense would run and how to guard
against them, he had just one final instruction before we were
done: "*Let's go f_ _ _ ing beat Michigan.*"

We did, 86–65. A. J. had 23 points and I had 19 points and
(probably a career high, sadly) 3 steals.

7

Hoosier Family Counseling

"Listen to Why Coach Knight Is Saying Something to You, Not How He Is Saying It"

Many of the IU players who had already graduated from Knight U with their basketball doctorates would come back and pass along this valuable piece of advice to the next generation of Knight players. (*"Who was that who made that pass? Haston!? It's been so long since you made a good pass I didn't know that was you."*) It was a great benefit to have them come back to Assembly Hall and take an interest in our success and development. The current players under Coach Knight felt a strong connection to the former Knight players, and vice versa. (*"Know the defensive rules, Haston! Get your head outta your a_ s!"*) It was a bond formed through a mutual understanding and appreciation for the work and time that each side knew the other had been through and/or was going to go through as a member of the Indiana Hoosiers' basketball program. (*"You have no idea what a kicka_ s attitude is!"*) All of these former players understood the mental and physical tests that were before us as we worked to play for one of the most demanding coaches in the history of the game. Their words of wisdom helped all of us better understand how we needed to approach the opportunity of playing basketball at Indiana University. (*"You're more of a Burger King All-American than a McDonald's All-American."*) I know their advice was much needed and used often during my first season as a player.

The first three games in the 1998–99 season couldn't have worked out much better. (*"When you're at home it wouldn't hurt to run some, just put your girlfriend about a mile in front of you."*) We beat Seton Hall in our first game and then turned around the next day with a 76–55 win against South Carolina, followed by a win in our home opener six days later against Indiana State (which had been so fired up to knock off their in-state big brother that they surged to a 19-point halftime lead). (*"That play you just made was about as useful as a rock with boobs."*) After a good "pep talk" by Coach Knight at halftime, we came back strong in the second half and rallied to win, 76–70. I ended up playing all twenty minutes of the second half, totaling 18 points and 16 rebounds for the game. It had been a long twenty-month wait to get back to playing meaningful games.

Waiting nearly two years between games gives one sufficient time to put things into perspective and to develop one's body and game. (*"What a dumba_ s freshman. Kirk, we don't expect freshmen to be able to pass until November anyway."*) I was fortunate Coach Knight had the patience to wait for me to become better prepared for the college game, and I was equally lucky that he had given me a chance from the very beginning of my first official season as a Hoosier. (*"Kirk, you're moving like you've got a pole stuck up your a_ s!*") Getting that opportunity in those first three games meant everything to me at the time, and I just wanted to do my best so as not to disappoint Coach Knight. My first season playing for the Hoosiers was off to a great start, but by the time the Big Ten Tournament came around at the end of the regular season, I found myself much closer to being a resident of Coach Knight's infamous doghouse than the penthouse. (*"You couldn't block that shot with a f_ _ _ ing tennis racket!"*)

It was at this time that the advice from all those former Hoosiers to focus on the "why" part of what Coach Knight was saying and not the "how" really helped me navigate one of the toughest mental tests that Coach Knight ever presented me. This par-

Knight Lines

HASTON! You gotta stop playing like a f_ _ _ ing boy scout!

—Coach Knight

Sophomore year, 10/28/98

ticular test came one day before we were flying to Orlando for what would be my first-ever NCAA tournament game in 1999. I had worked my way into playing significant minutes for Coach Knight in my first season of play, even earning a few starts along the way. Now, after hundreds of hours of working and competing, I was just two more practices away from our first-round NCAA tourney matchup versus George Washington University and my first taste of the "Big Dance." I felt like the NCAA tournament was at my fingertips, but by the time that evening's practice ended, I didn't know if I would even be allowed to dress out for the game. *"You've beat me. I'm whipped, you've won. Where do you want to go? Where do you want to transfer . . . [Two] f_ _ _ ing years of the same s_ _ t! You haven't improved any. So go somewhere a coach can get out of you what you can do because apparently I can't do it!"*

We had finished the regular season 22–9 and ranked no. 17 in the polls. Our final regular season game was a home win versus Iowa, a game in which I had suffered a broken bone in my left hand. This forced me to wear a cast for any activity on the basketball court. It was technically classified as a soft cast, though it was sturdy enough to protect the break in my hand from suffering any further damage if it took a direct hit. I got a few practices in with the cast before we headed to Chicago for our Big Ten Tournament opener versus Illinois. The doctor had cleared me to play because the break in my hand was located in such a place where there was no risk of injuring my hand any further. My performance, in what turned out to be an 88–62 loss against the Fighting Illini, had been horrendous. I think it had more to do with the weakness of my mind than it did with the pain in my hand. I had played timid and weak in my first Big Ten Tournament game. My lack of mental toughness had placed me squarely in Coach Knight's doghouse as we headed into our NCAA tourney preparations back in Bloomington.

One would be hard-pressed to find another coach in the history of the game of basketball who evaluated a player's practice performance as closely as Coach Knight did. A player who started and played great on Monday might get just 10 minutes of playing time in a game on a Friday if he had practiced like crap on Tuesday, Wednesday, and Thursday. Conversely, a player who had struggled in a game (as I had just done versus Illinois in the Big Ten Tourney) could pull himself out of the doghouse and earn another chance in the very next game by playing well in practice. It was one of the things I liked best about playing for Coach Knight (and by the way, this was the number one thing

I hated about playing for Paul Silas in the NBA). So I knew although I had struggled in the previous game, if I could perform well in the subsequent practices, I could still earn the opportunity to play significant minutes in the NCAA tourney.

The problem with my bounce-back plan was I hadn't mentally gotten to the point of trusting my hand. I was making too many stupid, soft mistakes in practice. These mistakes in practice weren't blatantly obvious and they probably would have gone unnoticed to a casual basketball fan, but when it came to Coach Knight's keen eye, every slightly mishandled catch of a pass or bobble of a rebound may as well have been accompanied with a siren and a big waving white flag. Coach Knight had seen enough of my regressing play to diagnose my current problem: lack of toughness. He wasn't sure if there was a fast-enough cure available that would have me ready to play at a level worthy of an NCAA tournament game. The combination of my poor play mixed with this being the next-to-last practice before we flew down to Orlando meant Coach Knight had the perfect opportunity to teach me a valuable lesson on toughness before my first NCAA tournament.

"HASTON! WHAT are you DOING? If you can't f_ _ _ ing play, get off the court! If your hand bothers you that f_ _ _ ing much, then just leave! [I just stood there on the court, waiting for 5-on-5 play to resume.] No, really, get off the court and start running the stairs. If you can't play any better than that, then just start running."

As I began the task of running up and down all 150 or so steps in the lower level of Assembly Hall, Coach Knight's evaluation of my play continued in a very loud manner. From the highest step of the lower level, all of the players and coaches on the court looked about the size of tiny Lego figures. However, even from this Assembly Hall altitude, Coach Knight's voice was still loud enough for me to hear every critical word about my "soft-a_ s play" in practice. I had made about four trips up and down the stairs when Coach Knight's ongoing critique turned into a direct command for me to follow:

"There is just no f_ _ _ ing way I'm dressing you out for George Washington. Just stop running and go to the locker room. I don't want you out here, and I don't want you here [practicing] tomorrow. You will not *dress out in Orlando. I'll take you down there, but I'm* not *playing you! Get out of here!"*

I heard my newly minted marching orders as I made my way down the steps toward the court where my teammates were still practicing at full pace. As I reached the lowest rows of Assembly Hall, I was at as low a place mentally as I had ever been since becoming a Hoosier. I knew that the way I had been playing in practice made me easily replaceable by a number of players on our roster. My first official dismissal from practice by Coach Knight couldn't have come at a worse time.

I took my hand cast off and left it for the trainer, then headed

Knight Lines

Sometimes you play with your head up your a_ s! Have you ever heard of a marmot? Well, it's a little animal about this big [Coach holds his hands about eight inches apart] and they dig up holes in the ground. Well . . . that marmot would have to go up your a_ s five feet sometimes to find your head when you play!

—Coach Knight
Freshman year, 12/1/97

to the locker room. It was still relatively early in our practice, and my teammates probably had about another thirty or forty minutes until Coach would end it. Missing any part of a practice was bad enough, but getting dismissed from a large portion of a practice right before the NCAA tournament was about as bad as it could get. This, even more than what Coach had just said, made it dawn on me that it was actually a real possibility I wouldn't play against George Washington. I felt pretty sure Coach wouldn't end up taking my uniform away from me, but I also thought he would take away all my minutes. As I entered the locker room, I knew that in addition to being squarely in Coach Knight's doghouse, I was on a very short leash as well.

I sank into the chair in front of my stall in the empty locker room. I just sat there by myself in silence for a few minutes. I was thinking that I had probably just thrown away my only chance to prove to Coach Knight that I was able and ready for my first ever NCAA tourney game. Since I had embarrassed myself enough in front of everyone for one day, I had no desire to be in the locker room when my teammates and coaches came into the locker room for the usual post-practice debriefing. I was in no mood to talk things out or to hear any pep talks from assistant coaches. My mind was on only one thing, and that was how best to exit the building as quickly and covertly as possible. As I sat at my locker, I contemplated whether I had time to both shower and change before the end of practice or if I should just change and take my stinky self back to the apartment so as to avoid anybody who had just witnessed my poor performance and subsequent banishment. But then in the midst of throwing this pouty pity party for myself, I came to the realization that my focus shouldn't be on the quickest Assembly Hall exit routes; it should be on how to make sure that my butt would be back on the court for our last practice in Bloomington before the tournament. I had let myself get bogged down in a checkers game when I was in the middle of a chess match. I needed to navigate myself from

Coach Knight's doghouse back into the playing rotation of the next game—and I had twenty-four hours to do it.

Of course, I had already witnessed one of my teammates earlier in the year not being allowed to practice by Coach Knight and then subsequently being told to exit Assembly Hall and not come back—the infamous tennis racket episode. I also was well aware that Coach had made sure this player didn't even *think* about coming out to practice because Coach had removed all of his practice gear from his locker stall before the player ever got to the gym. It was game over for me if that happened, so I had to come up with a strategy to counter what could have been Coach's next move.

Knight moves to locker room, captures practice gear . . .
checkmate.

I needed to protect myself so as not to be in the position of being unable to dress out for practice the next day. My next move was clear. If I was going to get back on the practice court, I had to have the gear to be able to do so. So I skipped taking a shower, changed back into my street clothes, put my sweaty practice gear I had been wearing in the laundry basket, and quickly got to work. I grabbed my sneakers, some shorts, and an old no. 35 practice jersey I had stuffed in the back of my locker stall from earlier in the season. Next, I bolted for the training room. I had left my other hand cast behind in the gym for our trainer, Tim Garl, but fortunately I knew that he had stored my backup cast in his bag in the training room. I hustled into the training room, where thankfully there was no sign of Garl, or anyone else for that matter. The clock was ticking: at any minute practice would be over and the entire locker room and training room area would be covered with players, coaches, and managers. I wasn't in the mood to hear anything, whether it was a pep talk or a continuation of the criticism I had just received. I grabbed my cast along with a roll of athletic tape and hurried back out into the hallway. I knew the perfect place for stashing my practice gear. There was a bathroom in the hallway between the training room and our locker room that was hardly ever used. I ducked into this bathroom and found a good hiding place for my collection of gear in the back of a shower stall. I was outside of Assembly Hall and inside my red Chevy Monte Carlo just a few minutes later—luckily never seeing a single person from the basketball program along the way.

Through the evening and the hours leading up to practice the next day, I hadn't heard anything from any of the coaches (which I felt was probably not a good sign). I got to Assembly Hall early enough to make certain that I didn't see any coaches, trainers, managers, or players on my way into the locker room area. I went straight to my bathroom hiding place, got dressed for practice, and used the athletic tape I had swiped from the training room to wrap my playing cast on as best I could with one hand. Next, I waited. I just hid out there in the bathroom and waited for the next forty minutes, trying to get as close to the time of practice as I could before going out to the court. My thinking was that it would be better to ask for forgiveness than permission. So I just stayed out of sight and didn't risk running into any of the coaches who might tell me to exit stage left if they had seen me walking around in my practice gear. When it was finally almost time for practice to start, I went down the hall (luckily evading detection) and through the locker room (where my locker had in fact been emptied) and made my way out onto the court.

I did my best to casually blend in with my teammates by shooting a few jumpers, at a basket that was as far away as possible from where Coach Knight was currently standing on the court. I did my best to act like it was just another day at practice (a move that *Seinfeld* creator Larry David would probably appreciate, since he once famously quit as a *Saturday Night Live* writer one day and then the next day just went back to work at the studios while pretending like nothing had happened the day before). As I continued to shoot, I kept stealing quick glances in Coach Knight's direction to see if he had noticed I was in the gym. Only a few minutes had elapsed when I could tell Coach Knight had noticed I was out on the court for practice (and that I was wearing practice gear that I wasn't supposed to have). Coach immediately signaled for Garl to come over to talk to him. I don't know for sure what Coach said to him, but my best guess is that it was something like "Why is Haston on the court—and how in the h_ _ l did he get practice gear?" Whatever their discussion was about, it was brief, and now Garl was walking in my direction. He sidled up next to me and said, "If you're going to practice, you need to at least come to the training room and let me tape that cast on the right way." I exhaled with a sigh of relief. I translated Garl's sentence in my mind to mean, "Coach Knight is going to give you one more chance today—so you better not screw this up."

I went on to have a great practice that day. Coach Knight took notice of my play and when our first-round game versus George Washington rolled around a couple of days later, he had me in the starting lineup in my first-ever NCAA tournament game. I

Knight Lines

You've proven you can play a lot of ways—
including like f _ _ _ ing dogs!

—Coach Knight

Junior year, 12/14/99

scored a then career-high 27 points on 9-of-11 shooting from the field and grabbed 9 rebounds in our first-round victory.

"Listen to *why* Coach Knight is saying something to you, not *how* he is saying it."

Maybe these aren't words to live by, but they were definitely words to play by.

Coach's Two Favorite Four-Letter "F" Words

Many people know that one of Coach Knight's favorite adjectives, nouns, and verbs is a certain four-letter "F" word that he's never been shy about using (just search "Coach Knight's Favorite Word" on YouTube for his own detailed explanation of why he likes to use the word so much). I've tried to keep most, if not all, cuss words from popping up in the pages of this book, but since this next story revolves so much around one particular four-letter word I'm going to have to approach this story timeout a little differently. For this story I'm going to assign a cleaner four-letter word in the place of the other four-letter word so that the story is a bit easier to read. For the sake of this story, let's just say that one of Coach Knight's favorite words is the word "PUCK" (as he states in the aforementioned YouTube clip, it's this word's versatility that makes it valuable to him since he can use it as a verb, noun, or adjective). This "puck" word really got some use at a practice during my junior year when our mild-mannered shooting guard, Luke Jimenez, found himself in the middle of a classic practice moment—and in the very middle of the Assembly Hall floor.

Luke Jimenez was exactly the type of person everyone would want as a teammate. He worked hard and was probably the most level-headed player on the team; as a matter of fact, he is probably one of the most level-headed people I've ever known. Jimenez was always a dependable voice of reason within our team. In the hundreds of hours I had spent around Jimenez at workouts and in practices, as well as playing hearts with him on road trips, I never once heard him say a behind-the-back comment about anybody else on the team, and very rarely did I ever hear him say a cuss word. Then one day in practice, in the heat of the moment, it happened. Jimenez made an uncharacteristically bad turnover and in his frustration at himself uttered a short, sharp, whisper of a yell under his breath as he turned to get back on defense on the other end of the court: "Puck!" Coach Knight was close enough to the action that he heard Jimenez's utterance and stopped practice almost immediately.

> Coach: *Luke, did that play you made just make you mad?*
>
> Jimenez: Yes sir.
>
> Coach: *Mad enough to say puck?*
>
> Jimenez: Yes.

At this point the rest of us on the court could tell that this was heading down an entertaining path.

> Coach: *Well, Luke, I've had some experience with that word, and I've learned that if you're going to say it—then you need to really f_ _ _ ing say it. If you're going to say "puck," Luke, then really say "PUCK"! Go ahead now, you try.*
>
> Jimenez: Puck.
>
> Coach: *D_ _ n, Luke, that's weak. If you're going to say it, say it where we can hear it.*

The entire team could barely keep a straight face—including

Coach Knight.

> Jimenez: **PUCK!**
>
> Coach: *Now that's better, but I don't think that person in the very last row up there could hear what you were saying.* [Coach gestures to a make-believe fan in the upper level of Assembly Hall]
>
> Jimenez: **PUCK!!!**
>
> Coach: *Now you're getting it. But I think you still need some practice. Go ahead and just stand there at half court, yell "puck," and keep turning around so that everyone in here can hear you.*

Jimenez, who was now standing right smack in the middle of the state of Indiana logo at center court, began to rotate clockwise while belting out a loud "Puck!" every couple of seconds, over and over again. With Jimenez otherwise occupied, Coach went ahead and inserted another player onto the white team to take Jimenez's place and then started practice again. We went right back into live five-on-five, full-court play. As we transitioned back and forth from end to end, we kept running right past Luke at center court, who was now spinning slowly around like a golf course sprinkler while yelling, "PUCK! PUCK! PUCK! PUCK!" with his voice reaching every corner of Assembly Hall. One of the team managers, David Pillar, told me later that he had started keeping track of how many "PUCKS" Jimenez belted out during his verbal exercise at center court, but lost count after a couple of minutes.

I know that most won't believe what I'm about to say, but I think there is a four-letter "F" word that Coach Knight used more often than "puck"—*film*. I couldn't believe how much film we watched at Indiana. My high school basketball coach had been a big believer in watching game film so we could see for ourselves what was and wasn't working. So I knew film work served an essential function inside a basketball program, but I didn't have any idea of the real significance of film until I was in the middle of my freshman year at Indiana.

My first glimpse into this new collegiate world of film study came when I walked by a room that was almost as large as our training room and was entirely devoted to the editing and dubbing of basketball film. Even by today's standards, it was a pretty elaborate set-up. Assistant coaches and managers would be assigned teams and games weeks in advance so they could get incredibly detailed scouting reports ready for a particular opponent. One could walk by that room at just about any point of the day and night, and there would be managers and assistant coaches in that room working on editing and taking pages and pages of notes on the film playing in front of them.

Game film wasn't the only film managers and assistant coaches were working on, either. One of the most vital parts of our preseason and pregame preparations was to go back and study film from our practices. Managers filmed all five-on-five action and kept stats as well. Coach Knight analyzed hours and hours of practice film on his own and then would have the key sequences edited together on one tape, which he would later show us in the locker room. During the season, the coaching staff would schedule time between classes for players to come in and watch film on specific players we would be guarding in upcoming games. Managers would also make each player a film of the opponents who played the same position on the other team. For example, if we were getting set to play Michigan State, then I would be sent home with a ten-minute video of Zach Randolph on offense and defense, while Mike Lewis would have a video of Mateen Cleaves and Charlie Bell. The best and worst part of film work was watching film with Coach Knight. The best was just learning what to look for and being able to see the game through Coach Knight's eyes as he explained and critiqued every last play on both ends of the court. The worst was being on the wrong end of the critique when it was you who had made a dumpster fire of a play on the big screen—although if it wasn't you he was getting after, it was a pretty enjoyable show to behold!

Once while Coach Knight was going over the previous night's game film with the entire team in our locker room, we saw A. J. Guyton miss a shot and immediately hang his head. Coach Knight paused the video and used his bright red laser pointer to highlight A. J.'s lowlight of a play. As the dot of the laser pointer focused on the top of A. J.'s head on the video screen, Coach Knight said, "*A. J., it looks like here you went on a blind date and when you went to meet her, you get there and find out that it's a fat-a_ s man.*"

Coach Knight treated film as the evidence he needed to properly prove a player's guilt or innocence when it came to the player's level of effort and execution on the basketball court. Sometimes Coach Knight didn't even wait for us to get back to the gym to use the film to become our judge, jury, and executioner. After a road loss, you never, *ever*, wanted to have your name called out on the team bus or plane, because that meant Coach had just seen something you had done wrong in the game film on the tiny little video screen of the hand-held camera. That's right, Coach didn't waste any time after losses. He would dive right into the game film and begin the process of trying to correct our mistakes before we had even cooled off from the game we had just played. I've had the dubious honor of being called up to the front of both the bus and the plane to watch my dumb mistakes on that tiny 4" x 4" screen.

"*Haston! Get your a_ s up here and watch your effort on this play*! [I begin the agonizingly slow walk in front of everyone like I'm off to the gallows.] *We spent all week talking about how to play this guy in the post, and I guess you just decided to say, 'F_ _ k that. I'll play him how I want to play him.' Is that what you told yourself? Just forget what I said and just do it how you want to do it? Is that what you decided? Because I sure as hell don't remember telling you to play defense like this. Does that look like how I told you I wanted you to guard this guy in the post?"*

There's no question that 99.9 percent of the time Coach Knight had you dead to rights when he called you out for a mistake. He normally didn't even need the video to pinpoint the exact moments that a player hadn't executed properly. He usually could remember every detail of the infraction. I learned to refrain from saying I thought he was wrong, because the film would inevitably prove that I had made the mistake he was telling me I had made.

Michael Lewis had the kind of personality to tell Coach Knight when he thought he hadn't made the blunder of which he stood accused. I'll never forget one such "conversation" the two of them had on the sideline of a Michigan game on January 6, 1998. In fact, their little sideline chat aired over all the sports highlight shows that evening. Coach Knight thought Lewis had not gone over a screen on defense like he was supposed to. Lewis thought he had made the correct defensive play and didn't shy away from sharing his point of view as he and Coach were walking next to each other toward the bench during a timeout. Nothing more was said about it in the locker room after the game by either one of them. It wasn't until the next day in our locker room before practice that Coach Knight walked in and began his talk with a direct message for Lewis.

"Mike, I don't mind being talked back to or being told something, but you better make sure you're right. Now I want you to go down there [to the film room] *and look at that play and come back and tell me if you were right or not. You had better make sure you're f_ _ king right next time."*

For Mike's sake, I was just glad this all happened in an 80–62 win over Michigan, because if it had been after a loss—then Coach Knight might have taken the whole thing *really* seriously!

8

This Is . . . Assembly Hall

On the evening of my first and only recruiting visit to the Bloomington campus, I was told to be at Assembly Hall at around 9:00 PM. Coach had been out of town but was going to be back at about that time and wanted me to meet him at Assembly Hall to show me around the place where I would be playing for the next four years. The parking lot was completely empty as I waited outside. I hadn't been waiting long when a SUV drove up and Coach Knight hopped out and headed toward me. Since I hadn't spotted him during his scouting trip to Clifton a few months before, this was the first time I had seen "The General" in person. My first impression was that I couldn't believe how big a man he was. I knew from seeing him so many times on TV that he was definitely not a small guy, but I really wasn't expecting him to be 6'5" and basically look at me eye-to-eye. Of course, there wasn't much small talk exchanged when we met. Coach was never one to dive into the "How are you doing, did you have a good trip?" pool of pleasantries. So with a quick pat to the back of my shoulder he said, "Let's go on in and take a look."

As we made our way down the steps to the court-level doors, my mind was racing. It would blow my friends' minds back home to know I was just taking a leisurely stroll through an empty Assembly Hall with the man that had made this place as legendary as he was. Coach Knight opened one of the large black double-doors and we walked onto the court. I looked down and could almost see my reflection in the shine of the hardwood beneath my feet. I took a long look around at the rows and rows of seats that steeply ascented toward the rafters. Not all the gym lights were on, so the darkness at the top of the arena made it look like the rows of seats never ended. "I can't believe the size of this place" were the only words I could muster as we walked over to the state of Indiana logo at center court. Coach replied, "It always appears to me a little smaller than it actually is on television." He was absolutely right about that. The camera angles the television crews use to shoot the games really don't do it justice, because I had always thought it looked like a 10,000-seat arena, but in actuality it has a capacity of more than 17,000. "And it's always sold out," Coach Knight added.

It was commonplace to walk into practice and see a couple of Major League Baseball players like Jim Thome and Robin Ventura hanging out, or one day walk by former Masters and U.S.

Knight Lines

We have to play like we're protecting
the last 25 years of Indiana basketball.

—Coach Knight

Junior year, 11/19/99

Open champion Fuzzy Zoeller at the Gatorade cooler. There was a pretty consistent line of visitors like Indianapolis Colts GM Bill Polian, Utah Utes head coach Rick Majerus, Indiana Pacers GM Donnie Walsh, and Chicago Bears head coach Dave Wannstedt. And of course, one of the consistent famous faces at Assembly Hall games is the hometown hero himself, John Mellencamp, who has had the same floor-level season tickets for decades.

I love those ESPN "This is SportsCenter" commercials that have random sports celebrities doing everyday jobs on the ESPN campus in Bristol, Connecticut. The one that has LeBron James wrestling with fixing the copy machine and the one that has Arnold Palmer making his famous "Arnold Palmer" sweet tea + lemonade drink in the ESPN cafeteria are a couple of my favorites. One of the incredible things about life in Assembly Hall was there were moments that were not unlike those that occur in "This is SportsCenter" commercials. Moments that made me pinch myself just to make sure that what I was seeing was actually real. One of these happened one day when I opened the doors to our locker room hallway about an hour before our scheduled team practice. I took two steps into the hallway, looked up, and saw an older gentlemen talking to a taller, younger man: Archie and Peyton Manning.

There's nothing like being greeted for practice by the most famous father and son quarterback duo of all time (sorry, Eli, but it's true). I tried my best to make small talk with the two of them—which, by the way, I failed at miserably. I could have kept it real simple and just told them it was nice to meet them, or that it was great to have them come visit one of our practices in Bloomington, or just wished good luck to Peyton and his Indianapolis Colts the rest of the season. I could have said any of those things. I should have said any of those things. But of course I couldn't just keep it short and simple. I had to try to be some sort of funny guy with Archie and Peyton. In hindsight, this was a poor decision. The only connection I could think of with the Mannings was Tennessee. "Hey, I'm from Tennessee and Peyton played college football at Tennessee!" This was the brilliant (insert sarcastic tone here) reasoning I had sorted out in my mind. And before I knew it, the following words were coming out of my mouth as I stopped in front of Peyton Manning: "It's good to have y'all here today. By the way, if you ever need a ride back to Tennessee from Indianapolis just give me a shout because I'm from there." Smooth as a pine cone. The look that Peyton gave me could be characterized as one part confusion and one part sadness. It was the same kind of look that parents give their five-year-old when the youngster has taken a knock-knock joke about four steps too far and reached the point of just saying that random animals and fruits are knocking on the door. "Thanks, I'll keep that in mind," Peyton somehow managed to reply without a hint of sarcasm. Well, at least I made an impression—not a good one, but an impression all the same.

I had another memorable moment with a legendary sports figure not too long after my awkward interaction with Archie and Peyton. This moment involved Hall of Fame and Olympic gold medal basketball coach Pete Newell. Even though Coach Newell retired from coaching in his mid-forties, he was far from done making an impact on the basketball landscape. Newell was the general manager of the Los Angeles Lakers from 1972 to 1976. During this time as the Lakers' GM he made quite a significant move in NBA history: he traded Junior Bridgeman, Dave Meyers, Elmore Smith, and Brian Winters to the Milwaukee Bucks for Kareem Abdul-Jabbar. Before his death at the age of ninety-three in 2008, Newell had become world-renowned for his legendary big man camps. This was a school he conceived and instituted and where he personally taught some of the game's greatest names how to develop their post skills—players like Hakeem Olajuwon, James Worthy, and Shaquille O'Neal.

The day that I was fortunate enough to share a few minutes with Coach Newell in our Hoosier training room, he talked to me about the "skill that all successful post players need to have," detailing for me the reasons why it was vital for a post player to be able to use both hands around the basketball goal and to cultivate the ability to go over either shoulder: so a post defender simply could not know until it was too late where the point of offensive attack was going to take place, the left side or the right. Then Coach Newell casually talked about a player that he had spent some time in the gym just watching practice: "There's a guy right now that isn't but 6'4", but he hardly ever gets his shot blocked because he uses both hands around the basket." He didn't name-drop, so I wondered who this "guy" was: turns out it was Charles Barkley, and the practices where Coach Newell had gotten a first-hand look at him were at Coach Knight's legendary 1984 Olympic trials at Assembly Hall. Coach wound up cutting the great Barkley because he didn't make a commitment to lose weight. (Maybe Coach should have left a tennis racket and a can of Slim Fast in his emptied locker stall.)

Coach Newell was a basketball visionary, the first coach ever to win the NIT, NCAA, and Olympic gold medal. Only two have managed the feat since: Dean Smith and Coach Knight. In the summer of 1974 Coach Newell sat in Coach Knight's living room and assisted him in the development of the revolutionary "motion offense." The level of respect that Coach Knight felt toward Coach Newell—generally revered as the greatest teacher of the post game ever—led to an incredible opportunity for Hoosier post players over the years. When Coach Newell worked with us, he would reiterate that "basketball is a game of counters: you counter the move the defense makes, and you do what the defensive man allows you to do." He went on to tell us that in order to be successful in the post, a player has to have the footwork and the wherewithal to recognize what avenue the defense was providing him to score. A basketball player can't predetermine his move any more than a boxer can predetermine exactly when and where he is going to throw a punch during a fight. The player and the boxer both have to recognize the openings, see the weaknesses in the defense, and then attack accordingly.

Coach Knight kept a close eye on our work, adding a few thoughts of his own to what Coach Newell was teaching us. But for the most part, Coach Newell took the lead in our instruction for the hour-long workout session. In the years I practiced for Coach Knight, this was the only time I would ever see him gladly let another coach take the lead in instructing his own players. That really stood out to me. Usually, if Coach Knight was on the basketball court with another coach, it was a natural thing for him to take the leadership role and it was equally understandable why 99 percent of basketball coaches would defer to him. Coach Knight held Coach Newell in such high regard that he had no problem trusting him on his court with his team, and there really wasn't a greater compliment that Coach Knight could pay to another coach than that.

An important step in my journey from redshirt practice player to a player Coach Knight could trust in the heat of a Big Ten battle involved a lesson taught by a pair of Knights—Coach Knight and his wife, Karen. In November of my sophomore season, Coach Knight and Ms. Karen came to me with a shot that they wanted me to try out, a shot that I had never used before a day in my life, except maybe in some random horse games on my backyard goal. The shot was the skyhook. My initial thought was, "The skyhook? Does anyone even use that thing in games anymore these days?" Coach Knight and Ms. Karen gave me the positives of the move and how they thought it would be a natural fit for me. It was just the type of go- to shot that a 6'9" white guy with long arms needed to get shots off over some of the long, athletic Big Ten post defenders that would be in my future. I was officially onboard with their idea to bring this throwback shot to Assembly Hall. There were a lot of growing pains that came along the way in learning this shot (not to mention the dozens and dozens of "Hey Kareem, nice shot" cracks I had to put up with from teammates). During the course of the next several weeks I took about 500 to 1,000 skyhooks per week. I had showed marked improvement with the shot in recent practices, and even though I was still not quite good enough at it to use it in real games just yet, Coach Knight apparently felt that I had mastered it enough to show it off to Coach Newell after one of the practices he attended.

Coach Knight announced that all the players should go to the locker room, take a shower, and change. Right after saying that, however, Coach Knight called me back over to the basket where he and Coach Newell were standing. Coach Knight had decided that he wanted to show Coach Newell my new skyhook shot that he had been teaching me. I think that Coach Knight figured that if anyone in the world would appreciate this particular shot, it would be a man who had personally worked with Bill Walton, a fellow with a lethal skyhook of his own.

I jogged in the direction of the two Olympic gold medal-winning coaches, feeling a tinge of nerves in the pit of my stomach when I heard Coach Knight tell me, "Go ahead and shoot a few hooks." For a good 10 to 15 minutes, one of our managers, David Pillar, fed me post passes as I would pivot on my left foot, fire my right knee up into the air while extending and swinging my right arm away from my body, and then allow the momentum of my body to cause the ball to roll off my fingertips toward the rim. Neither Coach Knight nor Coach Newell said much to me as I rolled these skyhooks at the basket again and again. While I shot and Pillar passed, the two Hall of Fame coaches stood close by and quietly analyzed my technique. Coach Knight instructed me to get my hand to a high finish on the follow-through while Coach Newell added some helpful comments about my footwork leading into my shots. Two Hall-of-Famers helping me learn one shot is about as good a tutoring situation as a basketball player could hope for. There were just some moments in Assembly Hall that I wish every basketball player had the chance to experience.

A Gator in the Hall

As I mentioned, we had several past Hoosier greats return to Bloomington to see Coach Knight and watch a practice and speak to the team in the locker room, as well as a variety of other noteworthy guests from the sports world who would make the trek to Bloomington for a visit. One memorable surprise guest that Coach Knight and our Hoosier team entertained was the Ol' Ball Coach himself, Steve Spurrier.

At the time Spurrier was the Florida Gators head football coach, and he was in town on a recruiting trip to see Bloomington High School South's star quarterback, Rex Grossman. Grossman was a top-25 recruit and a *Parade* magazine All-American, and he would be named Indiana's Mr. Football. While Spurrier was in town, he couldn't resist the chance to stop by and pay Coach Knight a visit and watch some of our workouts. As Coach Knight so often did with a lot of our esteemed guests, he invited Spurrier to come to the locker room after practice to meet the team and give us an opportunity to meet him. Coach loved having former players come back to speak to his current team, but he also enjoyed having other successful coaches impart some of their wisdom.

Knight Lines

The difference between an average player and a great player is concentration.

—Coach Knight

Sophomore year, 1998–99

As we all settled into our seats, Coach Knight would bolt into the locker room with his guest and proceed to give a remarkably detailed introduction of the person to the players, managers, and coaching staff in the modestly sized locker room area. One thing that Coach would often do as he wrapped up his introduction would be to give our guest speaker a little helpful nudge by providing him some sort of broad, sports-related topic on which to focus his short speech. So as Coach Knight was stepping aside and handing the floor over to Coach Spurrier, he simply said, "Steve, why don't you talk to the boys about concentration." The topic seemed like one that would be right in the wheelhouse for the renowned football coach. It wasn't beyond Coach Knight to put someone on the spot by throwing a Molotov cocktail of a topic at him before he was set to say a few words, but "concentration" was about as close to a soft ball that Coach Knight could serve up on such an occasion—or so we thought.

I don't know if Coach Spurrier had something else in mind to speak to us about or if he was just thrown off by the specificity of Coach Knight's topic. Perhaps he was just nervous to be speaking in front of the legendary Hoosier basketball coach. Whatever the reason, Spurrier was obviously flummoxed as he began to speak to us about what concentration meant to him. The following speech may not be verbatim, but it's pretty close to how it went that day for the Gator head coach: "*Well, boys, concentrating is something you need to do because it's good to have good concentration when you're focusing on something. Having concentration isn't easy but it's good if you can have it when you need it. Well, it was good to meet all of y'all and I wish you the best of luck this season.*"

No one in the room, not even Coach Knight, moved for a few seconds. It felt like we had just watched a *Saturday Night Live* sketch of Will Ferrell doing a mock–Steve Spurrier pep talk. It was the quickest and most confusing guest speech we had ever had. Coach Knight quickly jumped in and thanked Spurrier for his time and walked him back down the hallway. The team and the coaching staff all stayed where we were in the locker room, still a bit stunned by the abrupt talk we had just heard, and waited for Coach Knight to return to give us tomorrow's practice schedule. Only a couple of minutes had passed before Coach Knight returned to the locker room. The first words he said were,

"I sure didn't mean to stump him with that topic."

My mom, Patti
Kirk Haston, and
me, age two.

In my Lobelville
Hornet uniform,
8th grade,
1992–93.

Mom, Granddad, Granny, and me
with the state championship trophy
right after Perry County defeated rival
Columbia Academy in the TSSAA title
game, 82–47.

Playing for the Perry County Vikings
against one of our top district rivals,
Wayne County High School.

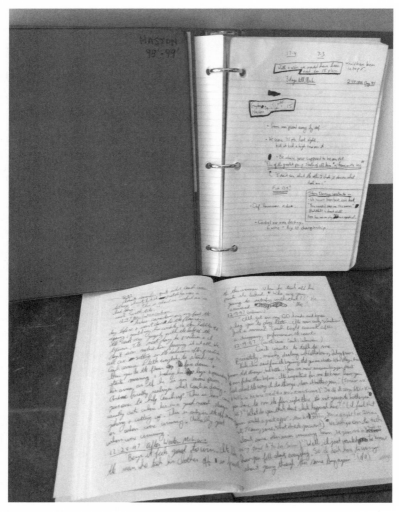

(This page and following) The red notebooks that Coach Knight required every player to keep notes in and have at every practice, game, and team meeting.

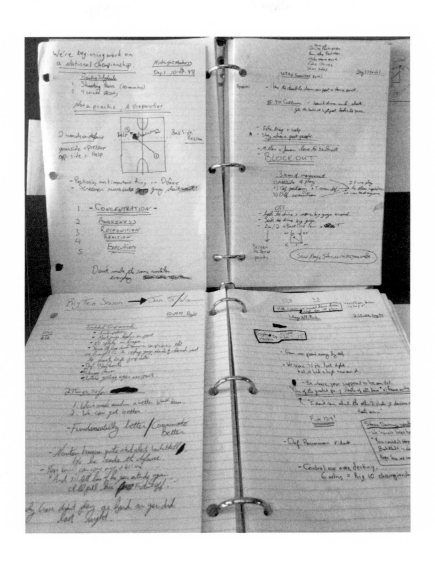

115

✳ TRUST THE RULES

Practiced
Good Passing !!

11-6-98 (con't)

- We have help off. + def.   ✳ Don't Pass to white
                                     Pass away from Blue.

It will let us get better.

Screen
Rescreen is
1st Priority.

- Open up w/ back hand in ● passing lane.

- Ball side = closed stance

● ✳ - Don't let Dribble over top.

Off.   - Worst Thing in Post Defense is
Spacing   Giving an angle.   ╱Awareness╲
Setup cuts   │ Alertness │
Screen Angles - Mental Intensity   │   +   │
Sharp Cuts   ╲Anticipation╱

- Immediately move to ball on pass out high or key.

Don't   ✳ Listening = Better Players
Leave   ✳ Communicating
Feet   ✳ See

              - listen to your eyes.
              - Help side ● lets you bump cutter.

● - Go under tomorrow → Ball screen high @ top of key
     Let's get this started tomorrow.

1 Day till NCAA's / GW   Day 123 3-10-99

Morning practice + leave at around 1:30 for Orlando.

NCAA / GW Gameday

Day 124 3-11-99

Matchups

A.J. → Rogers
Luke → King
Will → Machieroff
Larry → Nogongba
Kirk → Itube

" 1 Game, anything can happen."

"We can beat a hell of a lot of people."

- They look to run.
- Can't let Rogers penetrate.
- Cross screen / Down screen in post.
- Machieroff posts on left side of lane.
- Watch for tight cuts + ball screens + post flashes.
     Video of off post runs vs. Dayton
       - Post + dribble by Machieroff.

#1 Priority : Defense → Defensive conversion.
                           (Run the floor)

- Form shell around Rogers.
- Help from top (high post) on Machieroff.
- Call and switch.

Rogers / Machieroff / King

- Step out on ball side of screen.
- Post players are diving into post on ball screen.
     Off.
- Take Rogers inside   - Cross screen comes from opposite side AJ goes.

5 Years

3 Days till Kentucky 12-1-99 Day 39

3-0

Polls
#23

- We didn't play as badly as we played because ⬭ of their defense.

- We've all got to be tougher, can we all help Kirk,

- We're capable of being 4-0, 5-0, 6-0......

- last night @ 28 minutes we gave up 28 pts.

- The key to success in athletics is starting out on top.

- Only the lead dog sees the sunshine (French accent) the rest see a hole + dogs _ t.

Kentucky sets tape.

UK Personnel

#11 Smith - 6'2" pg. quick w/ball.
#22 Allison - 3 pt. shooter
#10 Boginz - driver 6'5"
#21 Prince - 6'9" LH shooter, LH driver
* BoxBot → #42 Magliore - 6'10" 250 Turns to middle of lane.
#3 Bevins - Spot up 3pt. shooter
#40 Cammara - 6'10" rather play outside Hawrick
→ #24 Stone - 6'9" Strong, reb, good passer

#5 ~~Knight Suite~~, screener, leather

118

Hoosier Classic

Holy Cross Gameday   12-28-99 Pg 59
                                  A.M.

9-1   Holy Cross Personnel
        # 10   ~~Wilson~~ : good shooter & defender
Off. Rebounder → # 35 Szatko : 6'8" Shoot open 3, ball screen/step back.
        # 22 Jerz : 6'1" 3 man, Quick, hits open shot.
Left Shoulder → # 40 Saukes : 7'1" Avg. 10 FT per game, No Angles.
        # 20 Sanchez : played 39 minutes last night.
        # 32 Kozium : good transition player.
        # 33 Stone : 3 3's last night.

        – Be solid in our stance & our
          pressure. No lunging & jumping.

        Be
        Smarter + Better   ~~~~~~
                                      P.M.

                   Matchups   Patience

Box + 1 =)   A.J. → ~~~~ Sanchez
Post exchange (◊) Jimmy → Wilson
   △   Mike → Jerz
Baseline Reverse   Lynn → Szatko   Left Shoulder.
   Zone = Pass Fake Kirk → Saukes : No Angles (Dead Behind Him
   Lynn & Kirk inside.   ★ Beat him   (Fight across lane
                                 to the spot.

                                      Shooters
– Don't help White on White.   Wilson
– Don't let him get to middle.   Szatko (52% 3 pt Line)
– Pressure on Passing lanes.

   – Effective Player/Team
        ↘ Best way to be described as a
                                    player/team

Matchups
A.J. → Crispin
Lynn → Stephens
Dane → Ivory
Newt → Smith
Kirk → Jackson

Def. Keys
Conversion
Post Def.
Driving Def.
3 pt.es by Crispin & Ivory
   Block out
   Ball Screen
TAKEAWAY BALL REVERSAL

"As a Coach you're like a parent, wanting
      to see you succeed."

"I don't get on your ass unless your worth it."

2 Days till Mich. St. #5   2-24-00 pg 106

"What's wrong with our team?"

Rules → Intensity / Attitude* / Confidence /

(All   Mental)   ← Aggressiveness /

Judgement

After game I.U.
" you're not a
good basketball player, but
you have a world of talent."

- "Minnesota & Ohio St. are the
games that concern me."

"everyone in this room has to improve
on something for us to be better."

('40, '53, '76, '91, '87)

"There's only 2 guys in this world that have
played on + coached a Nat'l Championship team, + I'm one of them."

"All in one season this team is among one of my
all time favorites and one of my most hated."
              All in one season.

1 Day till Mich. St.   2-25-00 Day 107

- Team player has rules in mind.
      Def. Points of Emphasis
1   Conversion Defense
2   Five guys on def. board.
3   Stay above Cutten
4   Switch b/w Granger & Peterson
5   Keep Ball on the side.

Meet your 2000–2001 Indiana Hoosiers. Immediately after our standard, serious team photo, we would do a silly team photo. (This is the serious one.) COURTESY IU ARCHIVES.

The Associated Press caption read: "Unranked Indiana's Kirk Haston, center, hits a three-pointer with time running out over Michigan State's Zach Randolph, left, to lift Indiana to a 59–58 win over the top-ranked Spartans in Bloomington, Ind., Sunday, Jan. 7, 2000. Michigan State's Jason Richardson is at right." ASSOCIATED PRESS/TOM STRATTMAN.

COURTESY IU ARCHIVES.

Just after my buzzer-beating shot!
COURTESY *HERALD TIMES*/DAVID SNODGRESS.

Putting an exclamation mark on an Assembly Hall
victory over Iowa in 2000.
COURTESY *HERALD TIMES*/ DAVID SNODGRESS.

Dane Fife (center) squeezing in and giving me and Jared Jeffries some late game advice. COURTESY *HERALD TIMES*/DAVID SNODGRESS.

Playing for the Charlotte Hornets during my rookie year, 2001–02.
COURTESY GETTY IMAGES/KENT SMITH.

9

Close to Greatness
& Close to Great Failures

I've been incredibly fortunate in my life to have spent a significant amount of time being close to greatness. Playing for Coach Knight put me in a position to learn many basketball and life lessons from one of the greatest coaches in sports history, and it has also provided me with the chance to learn from some other all-time greats of the game of basketball. I've had the opportunity to spend hours learning from men like Pete Newell, Mike Krzyzewski, Dennis Johnson, and Jerry West. I've had the chance to be in the same room with Bill Russell and hear his thoughts on the importance of competition. I've sat in the Duke Blue Devils' locker room in Cameron Indoor Stadium with Grant Hill and Christian Laettner and heard a Coach K pregame speech (it *was* a charity game, but nonetheless it was a very cool/ odd moment for a Hoosier to experience!). I've found myself playing in a pickup game in an old, rickety Louisiana gym (the kind that has an old stage located on one end of it) only to look up and see a legend walking in through the rusty gymnasium doors—a legend by the name of Larry Bird.

Knight Lines

It takes twelve years for a person to ever be called a doctor. It takes a helluva lot longer than that to become a good basketball player.

—Coach Knight

Freshman year, 10/1/97

One of my favorite examples of being close to greatness happened during my sophomore year when we were in Hawaii at a preseason tournament getting set to play Kansas State in our first game of the Maui Classic. One of the pregame team rituals that Coach Knight had us do when we were on the road was to have his long-time head trainer, Tim Garl, take us on a walk right before our final team meeting at the hotel. This walk usually took only about ten minutes and would normally consist of a route outside the hotel that Garl had scouted in advance. Seeing that we were in sunny, 85-degree Hawaii, we were looking forward to this walk much more than we had some of our walks on Big Ten road trips (nothing like an outdoor stroll in January while visiting Iowa City to play the Hawkeyes). On this day, Garl's little trek would take us out from the hotel, past the pool area, and down to the walkway that paralleled the beach. Tim's route choice was getting rave reviews from the team as we strolled past the pool. Let's just say that the scenery outside a Hawaiian beach resort is a little better than the parkas and scarves we were used to seeing on the campuses in Madison, Wisconsin, and Ann Arbor, Michigan. As we continued past the pool, we were somewhat startled by a booming "Good luck to you guys today!" from a large man lounging near the rail of the pool area. We all replied with meek thank-yous and head nods in response to the gentleman as we passed right by his deck chair. It's hard to muster up much more of a reply when you're talking to Magic Johnson for the first time.

Fresh off our first-round 71–70 victory over Kansas State, the coaches, managers, and players met in one of the hotel's conference rooms the next morning for breakfast and a team meeting as we got set to face Utah that day in the second round. Coach Knight had learned from Garl about our pregame brush with greatness the day before, and one of the first things Coach asked us in our team meeting was, "Why didn't one of you tell me you saw Magic? I'd have gone and gotten him to talk to you guys." The casual way that Coach said this wasn't done in a name-dropping kind of way (unlike what it sounds like every time I try to angle one of my Magic, Michael, Bird, or Isiah stories into my personal conversations). Coach said this about Magic in a way that made it seem as though he was some neighbor who had come over for backyard cookouts in the summer.

Ten hours later at our next team meeting I was shaking hands with Magic Johnson. Before we left the team meeting he told all of us, "Remember the love of the game and *always* play with your heart."

The athletes who occupy the upper echelon of sports' greatness are the one percent of the one-percenters. Unfortunately, most of us will never know what it feels like to be in this category of greatness. We won't ever know what it's like to come from nothing and achieve everything in a sport. We won't know what it feels like to be an MLB, NBA, or NFL superstar. We won't ever have a Nike or Gatorade commercial, and we will never get to say that we're "going to Disney World" as we're hoisting the Lombardi Trophy at the Super Bowl. Conversely, most of us will never experience the extreme lows the all-time greats have to endure. Most of us will also never experience what it feels like to be the all-star athlete who fails to hit the pitch, catch the pass, or make the shot for a championship in front of millions of people—many of whom can't wait to call him or her "a choker" or "gutless" in the immediate aftermath of this moment of failure. Most of us will also never know what it's like to be a person at the height of his/her profession who suddenly hits rock-bottom in a very embarrassing and public manner, losing their fame, fortune, and reputation at the hands of drugs, alcohol, or even a Perkins Pancake House waitress (Tiger Woods maybe can read a green, but wow, did he ever misread that whole deal!). These types of extreme highs and lows may be what fascinate us, but it's usually pretty far from what most of us will ever experience.

My experience of being close to all-time greats like Coach Knight has been an enjoyable part of my life. The same, however, cannot be said about what it's like being close to achieving great moments, only to ultimately suffer the feeling of great failure. This can lead to a lot of nights being haunted by the ghosts of close-calls past. Being close to achieving great moments is a double-edged sword. It's a remarkable feeling of achievement to make a run to a championship with a team, but it's a feeling that subsides quickly and cruelly if you and your teammates aren't holding up the championship trophy in the end.

Being so close to these great moments can have a purgatory-like feeling because you find yourself so close to reaching your goal of a championship, but instead you find yourself right there on the field of play as your opponents celebrate the victory you were striving so desperately to achieve. While playing for the Hoosiers, our teams consistently achieved high national rankings during the season, but one of my biggest regrets was never being a part of a Big Ten championship team. The closest we came was in 2001 when we made a deep run at the Big Ten Tournament title. In the semifinals of that tournament we faced the fourth-ranked Illinois Fighting Illini at the United Center in Chicago in front of 23,418 fans. It was a back-and-forth game that came down to the final play, but in the end we came out with a two-point victory. That 58–56 semifinal win led us to the conference championship game versus Iowa, where my three-pointer from the top of the key was deflected by the outstretched hand of future NBA player Reggie Evans. As my shot fell short, so did our attempt at bringing a Big Ten title home to Bloomington. Final score: 63–61. Moments like this led to a swelling sense of disappointment as we thought about that great moment we were just on the cusp of experiencing.

The result of such difficult moments can impact a player (or coach) in a couple of very different ways. It can have a negative effect on his or her level of desire and confidence. Or it can lead to numerous positive benefits in the form of learned lessons on humility, self-awareness, and highly motivated work ethic. You can either make these close-to-great moments feel like mile markers that you pass by as you drive toward improvement, or you can treat them as detours from which you never get back to the main road while you stray further and further from achieving success again.

Being part of sports is a humbling experience. Sports can teach us valuable lessons in humility by forcing us to come face to face with failure—over and over again. If you are going to choose to play a sport for a long period of time, you better get accustomed to working through disappointment if you plan on enjoying any future successes. The last ten years that I played basketball I was constantly dealing with crushing disappointments. I was fortunate to enjoy a few great moments, but the inevitable flipside to those great moments are the memories of the many almosts, what-ifs, and close calls along the way. Experiencing failure can either teach you how to handle loss and truly appreciate the successes you do achieve, or it can lead you to being close to miserable. These are by no means mutually exclusive categories. It's easy for the most level-headed, optimistic people in the world to sometimes drift near the misery side of the equation if they start throwing pity parties for themselves by focusing on regrets for too long. One of the great benefits of sports is the lesson on humility it teaches. And trust me, if there was ever a group of people who needed some quality lessons on humility, it would be athletes and coaches. Some of the cockiest know-it-alls on the face of the earth can be found in the world of sports. (I think all the rest are either in politics or on the set of ESPN's *First Take*.)

Ghostbuster Granddad

My junior season in high school was the third consecutive year that our team had made it into the TSSAA State Tournament, held in the Murphy Center at Middle Tennessee State University in Murfreesboro. We were 28–2 and ranked no. 1 in our classification as we entered state tournament play in the Elite Eight round of play. We played well enough in the first two games to advance. Then, in the finals, we had the state title all but wrapped up versus Boyd Buchanan, a 30-win private school from Chattanooga, when we missed a couple of free throws and then they hit a clutch three-pointer in the last 15 seconds of the game, and suddenly we were left with a one-point deficit and 1.5 seconds on the clock.

We should have already lost the game by then. Trailing 48–47 with 5 seconds to go, we had the ball and were inbounding it on the baseline under our opponent's basket. Our inbounds passer (who was also the starting catcher on our baseball team) reared back like he was about to gun down a runner attempting to steal second—but he showed off his arm a little too much. He over-shot the outstretched arms of the intended recipient of the pass (which was me) at the half-court line by a few feet. We were attempting to complete the play later made famous by Valparaiso's Bryce Drew (who, ironically enough, would be my Charlotte

Hornets teammate five years later) in their game versus Ole Miss in the 1998 NCAA Tournament. The ball was too high for me to get a hand on it, which allowed a Boyd Buchanan player behind me to intercept the pass. The Boyd Buchanan player then began to celebrate by tucking the ball under his arm and running to the other end of the court with his free hand high in the air as he did his best Deion Sanders high-step impersonation. The only problem for him was that there were still two seconds left on the clock when he intercepted the pass. The whistle blew and the referee called the poor kid for traveling.

This gave us a second chance for an inbounds play (this time from half-court) with about a second left on the clock. This time the inbounds pass was on the money. The play was for the in-bounds passer to throw a lob close to the paint that I could catch and shoot in the air because there was probably not enough time to come down with the ball and go back up for a shot before the clock expired. But the player guarding me anticipated the pass and jumped for the ball at the same time I did. I was able to get to the ball and catch it, but the defender had timed his jump in such a way right in front of me that I wasn't able to get a shot off while I was in the air. I had to come down to the floor and then try to get a shot off as quickly as I could around my defender

Knight Lines

In today's world if you have any competitiveness, you'll be successful.

—Coach Knight

Freshman year, 2/23/98

before the horn sounded. My defender and I landed just outside the paint, near the right block on the post. I angled past him and from about 5 feet away got off a floating shove of a shot at the rim as quickly as I could. The ball hit the side of the rim nearest me and went straight up in the air. As the ball hovered over the circle of the rim, the red light on the backboard lit up and 0.0 showed on the clock. The ball arced forward and then softly bounced onto the other side of the rim, on its way to officially becoming a missed field goal by no. 35 of the PCHS Vikings. It's about as close as a team can come to being a state champion without being one. The opportunity to make that day a special moment for my team and my hometown had been in my hands and I failed to come through for everyone when it had mattered the most.

After the awards presentations, I walked off the Murphy Center court and to our locker room with my teammates. All of our heads were down, not paying much attention to our well-meaning fans in the stands yelling the usual platitudes like "We'll get 'em next year, guys." That idea may have been directed at players like me, since I had one season left in high school, but it didn't offer much comfort to our senior players who had just poured their hearts out for thirty-three games that season. For the first time in my life, I walked into a basketball locker room with tears in my eyes. I looked down and saw in my hands a plaque that read, "1996 Class A State Tournament MVP." Those words couldn't have been any farther away from describing how I felt, however. I walked down to the far end of the locker room, stepped into the empty shower area, and did my best Clayton Kershaw impression, fast-balling my MVP plaque into the concrete wall. I quickly got dressed and rode back home with my mom. It was a long ride home after that loss and it was even a longer night. That night was the first time I had a good night's sleep haunted by a ghost of close-calls past. I'd just had the opportunity to deliver a state title to our tradition-rich basketball community and failed. I didn't realize it at the time, but the crushing pain that came from that moment was the second most important thing that ever happened to me as a basketball player. The *most* important thing that ever happened to me as a basketball player came the very next day.

The day after our loss in the state championship game, Granddad came to visit Mom and me in Lobelville. Besides being a minister for over thirty years, my granddad has had a couple of other notable career achievements. He had an impressive college and semi-pro athletic career, playing both basketball and baseball at David Lipscomb College (now Lipscomb University) and was even invited to spring training with the old New York Giants (his family needed him to stay at home and work on the farm, so he was unable to attend). He was also a professor at Freed Hardeman University for thirty years and was the head basketball coach there from 1963 to 1976. The other "profession" that he occupied was being my own, personal basketball coach. From the day I was old enough to stand up and shoot a Nerf basketball and all the way through every high school basketball season, he did an incredible job getting me prepared to play the next game. Even though there were no more games left to play that year, Granddad thought it would be a good idea for me to extend my junior season one more day by having one more workout. Granddad had always told me that he would never make me work out, but that anytime I wanted to go he would go with me. He wanted me to be self-motivated and not forced into it. That said, if I ever started to ask, "Hey Granddad, do you think we should go—" he would usually be out the door with the gym keys in his hand before I could finish the question. But in all the years of gym workouts he and I had done together, this was the only time I ever remember him taking the initiative and telling me that I needed to get off the couch. He walked in and just said, "Let's go get some shots up." I guess Granddad recognized a teaching moment when he saw one, so we headed down the road in his red pickup truck to the outdoor basketball court at Lobelville Elementary.

It was on that afternoon, while shooting at an old rusty rim on that outdoor court, that my granddad taught me several important lessons. He taught me that it was a good thing when a loss hurt that badly because it showed how much the game of basketball meant to me. He taught me that when you're faced with an obstacle, working on your game isn't an option if you want to overcome that obstacle—it's a necessity. He taught me that the hope for success is born out of the feeling of failure. And finally, my granddad taught me that the most important thing you can do for someone who is going through a tough time is simply to be there for them. I've really been blessed to always have a man like my granddad there to help me handle both my failures and successes.

> Coach Knight: You know *how* to play basketball. Where did you learn to play?
>
> Me: From my granddad.
>
> *At my first individual meeting with Coach Knight, 11/5/97*

10

Let the Games Begin

It was November 6, 1998, twenty months since I had played in a real basketball game, and that had been as a high school senior. Coach Knight told the team before our opener with Seton Hall how "important it was to get our season started off well," and that we must play with good "balance and position" if we were going to begin the season with two victories (the second matchup would be the next day against South Carolina, both games part of the National Association of Basketball Coaches Classic). Coach had us write in our red notebooks the following information to remember as we neared that first game:

1. Remember to stick to our defensive rules.

2. Play the passing lanes on defense.

3. Stay above our man on defense.

4. Don't allow ball handlers to split us on the perimeter.

5. Have good low, short recoveries on defense with no over-commitments.

I left the meeting and headed up the elevator to my hotel room where I gave my mom and granddad a call. They were making the six-hour drive from Tennessee so they could be at my first college game. I really had some reservations about them making that kind of drive to see the game since I had played very few possessions in practice on the red team (which was always the main unit in practice) and had no real expectations this would change come game time. There was a distinct possibility the only shots and rebounds they might see me make in the season opener would be in the layup lines during pregame warm-ups. However, I knew it didn't matter what I thought or said; my mom and granddad had their minds set. They were going to be there for my first game even if it meant I was doing exactly what they would be doing at the game, sitting. The only difference would be that my seat had a better view and I would be wearing candy-striped warm-up pants.

On the day of the game, Coach Knight wrote the names of our starters on the white board in the RCA Dome locker room. It was no surprise that they were the same guys that had been getting most of the reps on the red team in practice. A. J. Guyton, Luke Recker, and Dane Fife were the starting guards, and Lynn

Knight Lines

You're f _ _ _ ing lucky to have [this chance] in your lives . . . You better not p _ _ s it away!

—Coach Knight

Sophomore year, 1998–99

Washington and Will Gladness were the starting forwards. After a few more last-minute instructions from Coach Knight, we headed down the long dome corridor toward the court entrance and stopped at a spot that was just close enough to see some of the crowd, but far enough away that none of the crowd could see us. As we huddled together and readied ourselves to run out onto the court, the butterflies in my stomach felt like they were riding rollercoasters. We began our jog onto the RCA Dome floor, above which between 15,000 and 20,000 fans were waiting to watch the game, including two family members of mine.

As our pregame warm-ups came to an end, my mom and granddad settled into their seats for what they thought was going to be a relaxing afternoon. My mom had always found my games pretty stressful. It wasn't unusual to look over and see Mom in the stands with her head buried in both hands, peeking through her fingers in a way that made it look more like she was watching a scary movie than a ballgame. After the Seton Hall game, Granddad told me that about four minutes into the first half Mom had turned to him and said, "It is kind of nice to just be able to come to a game, sit back, and not have anything to really worry about." Then, just when the last words of that sentence were coming out of her mouth, Coach Knight stood up from our bench, pointed in my direction, and sent me to the scorer's desk to check into the game. From that moment on, she was back in her usual game mode, which was one-half worry and one-half excitement. What she had thought was going to be two hours of a relaxed basketball game for her, just cheering the players and eating popcorn, had quickly turned into a couple of hours of focused basketball watching and Tums chewing.

Led by our preseason All-American A. J. Guyton (23 points) and junior Will Gladness (16 points, 14 rebounds, 5 assists), we defeated Seton Hall 83–69. I contributed 17 points and 8 rebounds in 27 minutes of heartburn-inducing play (to my mom) to our winning effort. Chris Broussard (who now works for ESPN) covered the game for the *New York Times* and wrote that "within minutes . . . the Indiana Hoosiers played the role of teacher and, with all the tenderness of a military commander, forced the Seton Hall Pirates into the role of the aggravated pupil. [Indiana] tutored their guests on the finer aspects of hard-nosed, fundamental basketball." Tommy Amaker, the Pirates' head coach, probably summed up the game the best: "Their defense was suffocating. It was aggressive. It was all of the things when you think of Indiana basketball and Coach Knight" (Broussard; see bibliography).

My granddad loves to tell the story of what happened right after the game was over. A gentleman who was an Indiana fan had been sitting near my mom and granddad, and over the course of the game he had been able to deduce that they were my family. As soon as the final buzzer sounded, the gentleman made a beeline for my granddad with his game program in hand. After he got close enough to get my granddad's attention, he pointed to something on the roster page of the program and asked my granddad with deep curiosity, "Where exactly is this *Lobelville*, Tennessee?"

If I had never gotten off the bench or had just played a few minutes, my mom and granddad would still have thought their six-hour drive north was worth it. But considering that I not only played but helped contribute to the win, they were ecstatic and stunned at how the evening's events had unfolded. I remember after the game coming back out to the stands to visit with them for a few minutes before the team got on the bus and headed back to the hotel. The first thing my mom did was hug my neck. She didn't say much of anything before or after she hugged me, but the look on her face told me how proud of me she felt. I know that night was a special moment for all of us. After all the time of being away from home and unable to play basketball in front of my mom and granddad for over a year, I was finally able to show them tangible proof that their belief in me over the years was beginning to pay dividends on the court.

The Mom with the Plan

I was in seventh grade at Lobelville Elementary and I was excited about getting my new uniform for the Lobelville Hornets' 1991–92 basketball season. Most of the seventh and eighth graders got to pick their uniform numbers, but when you are a 6'1", 180-pound twelve-year-old, you just get assigned the biggest uniform available regardless of number. After I got my jersey, I hurried to the boys' bathroom to try it on. I was anxious to see myself in it as soon as possible. But my heart sank when I put my uniform on for the first time. None of you probably know this, but that very day in the boys' bathroom at Lobelville Elementary I basically invented the form-fitting, compression athletic shirt that has since made Under Armour famous.

In seventh grade my physique was far more Phil Mickelson than Dwight Howard. As I looked at myself in the bathroom mirror, I noticed that the tight-fitting jersey wasn't leaving much to the imagination. For me, then, it felt like the end of the world having to wear a tight, form-fitting jersey on a sweatshirt kind of body. I had quickly gone from looking forward to the start of the basketball season to absolutely dreading being on the court looking like I did.

When I got home, my mom wanted to see my new basketball uniform. I grudgingly went to my room and put it on again, pretty much having to hold my breath in order to do so. Soon I appeared in my ill-fitting uniform and she of course said it looked fine, as any good mom would say, but she could tell how uncomfortable and embarrassed I was about it. I knew I had to lose weight, but there's nothing worse than the moment when something happens that puts your biggest insecurity on display for everyone else. Mom stayed positive and told me that I shouldn't worry about it. Of course, she knew me well enough to know that I was definitely going to worry about it and be miserable all the way up to and through the upcoming basketball

Knight Lines

You are the captains of your fate and the mothers of your destiny.

—Coach Knight

Junior year, 12/18/99

season. Luckily for me, though, my mom had a plan to help me, as usual.

The long-term solution of getting in better shape and losing weight wasn't of tremendous use in the short term. It was just a week before the beginning of basketball season. It was a time when a middle-schooler playing basketball should have been filled with excitement, but for me it was an occasion filled with nothing but anxiety. Then, just a few days before our first game, my mom came home with something that changed everything for me. She had in her hands my maroon Hornets jersey. She told me to go try it on. As I put that jersey back on, I noticed it now fit and even had a little breathing room! My mom, ever the problem solver, rarely a problem creator or complainer, had come up with the short-term solution that I thought didn't exist. My mom had found a seamstress in town and had her sew in two inches of maroon fabric on either side of my jersey.

With this simple solution, Mom had eased my worries about the start of the season and gotten me back to a place where I was excited about playing basketball. Mom knew I loved the game, and that I wouldn't be at my best if my confidence was shaken because I was worrying about the way I looked. This was just one example of many where my mom helped me prepare for challenges. I knew I had a lot of work to do on my end to make her actions worth the time and effort. If I was going to play basketball in high school, I knew I had to get my body and my game better prepared. Besides, if my mom had to stitch up the seams of one of my high school jerseys, my teammates would probably have never ever let me live it down!

11

Phone Call

*F*or my sophomore year Mom, Granddad, and Granny decided to become my roommates in Bloomington, at least
occasionally. They paid half the rent on my apartment, which
had a second bedroom available and a futon in the living room,
enough space to give them a great place to stay during their fre-
quent trips to Bloomington. Since I had been spending most of
my down time at the apartment of my good friends Brandon
Sorrell, David Pillar, and Ted Hodges, who were managers on
the basketball team (I usually just called their place BDT's, for
short), it really didn't bother me not to have a roommate. Most
days I would just come back to my apartment at about 11 PM
and go right to sleep, and I really liked having a guaranteed quiet
place for studying and sleeping when I needed it. But the one
downside was that if my alarm clock failed to work for some
reason, I didn't have the safety net of a roommate to make sure I
was out of the door on time.

I was absolutely terrified of oversleeping when I was in college (I still have nightmares to this day about oversleeping and
being late to Indiana practices or games). Just the thought of

being late for one of Coach Knight's practices had gotten me into the habit of setting multiple alarms every time I lay my head on a pillow. I would set my primary digital alarm clock along with a backup wind-up clock. Then I would set a back-up to my back-up (like I said, I was pretty paranoid about being late or missing a practice). The last step in this alarm clock ritual was to give my mom a call and ask her to phone me at a certain time to make sure that I was up. (No, my one-pound Nokia flip phone didn't have an alarm feature way back then.)

On Wednesday, May 5, 1999, I was close to officially finishing my sophomore year at IU. It was the last day of my final exams, and I was more than ready to head back to Tennessee for a rare extended stay at home. The day began the same way many of my college days had, with a call from my mom to make sure I had gotten up. In this case it was also to make sure that I was out of the door on time in order to get to my last two final exams. Mom's usual "Good morning, son. Are you up?" greeted me on the other end of the line. I said yes and she wished me good luck on my tests and wanted to know when I would be coming home. I told Mom my plans were to come home the next day, on Thursday morning, but my actual intentions all along were to leave Bloomington right after my last exam and head for home late Wednesday afternoon and surprise her that night. It was a 350-mile drive that took about five-and-a-half hours. If all went according to plan, I figured I could leave in time to get home for Wednesday night Bible study and that way surprise Grand-dad also. Our conversation only lasted a couple of minutes as we both had classrooms to get to, hers at Lobelville Elementary and mine on IU's campus.

After I completed my first final exam that morning, I decided to hang out on campus rather than drive back and forth to my apartment. I went to the Kelley School of Business library to kill some time and also to get a little more studying in before my next test. I felt pretty confident about the exam, but then I

Knight Lines

Develop a heart that won't allow you to be beat.

—Coach Knight

Junior year, 1/22/00

found an unexpected test right there in the library, and I didn't feel nearly as confident about this one. This test was in the form of a cute brunette who had just walked in and sat down at the table a few seats from where I was sitting. After more than a few minutes of giving myself a pep talk about going over and talking to her, I decided to make it into a self-challenge and go over and ask this girl out. A self-challenge is basically the equivalent of a triple dog dare in the move *A Christmas Story*. In other words, there was no turning back now! I had convinced myself that if I didn't complete this challenge, then I was nothing but a down-right gutless coward. My mind was made up. Now I just had to get my legs and words to do their part or I was going to feel like a failure the rest of the day. I gave myself one more mental pep talk: "Come on, you coward, don't act like a wimp! You're a Hoosier basketball player—now go over there and at least *pretend* you've got some game *off* the court!"

I spent the better part of the next ten minutes pretending to look at books on the shelves around our table (OK, who said pep talks have to work quickly?). As confident as I felt about my up-coming final exam, I was equally apprehensive about talking to this girl. I kept going over possible things to say while pretending to peruse books that, for all I knew, might be upside down in my hand. Making matters even worse, there was now a guy who had taken a seat just one down from the brunette. If I was going to attempt a "cold call" conversation with this attractive coed, I definitely didn't need this guy or anyone else within earshot of a possible crash-and-burn situation. I was not only fighting a battle against my nerves and the clock (I only had about five minutes until I needed to leave for my exam), but now I had to deal with this random dude. Luckily, with just a couple of minutes to spare, he finally took off and thus left me with no more excuses. I put the book (that I was pretending to read) back on the shelf, walked back over to the table, and sat down right across from her.

I took a deep breath and then dropped probably one of the most debonair lines in pickup history: "Excuse me, my name's Kirk. You probably have a boyfriend, but if you don't, I wondered if it'd be OK if I gave you a call sometime?" BAM! Totally nailed it! Take THAT, Dos Equis Most Interesting Man in the World! Someway, somehow I got her phone number. Just a few hours into my day and I had one exam done, one future date set up (though in the days to come I would lose the number that I had worked so hard for), and only one more exam to complete before I was heading home for a couple of weeks of summer break. Little did I realize at the time that the path I thought my near future would take would soon become a journey that would change my life forever.

The first part of my near future that didn't go as I had initially planned was my departure date for home. I ended up deciding not to go through with my first idea of driving home after my last exam that day, and decided to stay in Bloomington one more night before heading home the next morning. One of the reasons was that there were some strong storms forecast for the south and parts of the Midwest as well. Another reason was that it was going to be the last night I was going to be able to hang out with a lot of my friends for quite a while. Many of them would not be coming back for summer school. So as soon as I got done with my last exam I headed over to BDT's place.

I might as well have had my mail delivered to BDT's considering the amount of time I spent at their Hoosier Court (now called Regency Court) apartment on South Henderson Street. As the evening approached, storms began to roll into the Bloomington area. At around 7 PM, I told my friends that I would be back in a little bit as I headed out to a nearby Church of Christ on East Hillside Drive for a midweek Bible study. I pulled up to the small hill where the church sat, parked my red Chevy Monte Carlo with its IU35 license plate, and hurried through the driving rain to the church entrance.

What I didn't know what that as I was dealing with the storms in Bloomington, my mom and other members of her church back in Linden, Tennessee, were readying themselves for some strong storms of their own.

Mom often went to a midweek Bible study at the Church of Christ in Linden. That night, word moved quickly among the congregants that an abnormally strong cell of storms was moving through the area. It didn't take long after Bible study was over for everyone to quickly find shelter so they could wait out the extreme weather threatening to come through middle Tennessee. Since our house in Lobelville was about fifteen minutes north of Linden, Mom decided to take shelter at the house of a longtime family friend, Hollis Hinson, only about a mile away from the church. By the time they reached the house, both television and radio reports were warning residents to take immediate shelter because a tornado in the area was now considered likely. Tornadoes are generally very rare in my home county (it had been over twenty years since the last one had touched down there), but the warnings made it clear that residents should take all proper precautions. Since the house had no basement, Mom and Hollis took shelter in a windowless bathroom in the innermost part of the house. As they waited there, a severe thunderstorm began to rage outside.

In Bloomington, the rain had let up considerably by the time I got out of church. I headed back to BDT's, where I spent the next few hours watching TV and talking with my friends about their summer plans. It was just like a hundred other nights I had spent in college, except for one thing: I never got a single call from home on my cell phone. That was a bit out of the norm, but I just figured that the bad storms in the area had affected the cell reception. I left BDT's apartment around 11:45 PM. The parking lot was pretty damp, but the rain had finally stopped. With summer break knocking at the door, the entire apartment complex was quiet and the parking lot was much emptier than usual. I got in my car and began the ten-minute drive back to my apartment, where I still needed to get some packing done before my trip home the next morning.

A lot of kids who grow up in a place like Lobelville can't wait for the day they can get away from their one-horse town. But going off and living hundreds of miles away from your friends and family is enough to make even the most cynical kid miss home. So for someone like me, who loved my hometown, it was always grueling to wait out the weeks and months between trips back there. This was partly on my mind as I got back to my apartment on East 10th Street close to midnight, but I was still wide awake and ready to pack up for the long drive about eight hours later. I unlocked my door, walked in, and immediately noticed that the message light on my answering machine was blinking. I tossed my keys onto the table and pressed the play button. It was Granddad. All he said was to give him a call as soon as I got the message, "no matter how late." I also noticed I had a lot of missed calls on my caller ID from Tennessee numbers, but the only message on the machine was from Granddad. I was still standing in my small living room when I began dialing Granddad's number. He answered quickly. I said, "Hey Granddad, I just got your message and was givin' you a call back." He began to talk, but his voice was softer than usual, and it had a tremble in it that I had never heard before.

"Son . . . there was a storm . . . a tornado hit here . . . we lost your mom . . . Patti is gone."

By the time my granddad had finished a sentence that no father should ever have to say about his own daughter, I had dropped straight down to my knees. All I could say back into the phone to Granddad was "*No . . . no . . . no*" over and over again.

My face was wet with tears. As I tried to catch my breath, Granddad gathered himself quickly. He began to talk to me calmly, his voice back to its usual, strong tone. As a preacher, for years and years he had been the one who comforted others, the one who tried to give others strength in their time of sorrow, sickness, or tragedy. Even at a moment when he had lost his only child, he didn't allow himself to be the one who needed comforting when there was someone else who needed it more. His faith and the role he had accepted in life meant that he had been the strong one in the room hundreds of times, for hundreds of people, at too many hospitals and funeral homes to count. Still, this was different: the first time he had to be this type of helpmeet for his only grandchild. Granddad knew the bond my mom and I had, he knew I was going to be overwhelmed with grief, and he knew he needed to do everything he could to help me make it through this tragedy.

Granddad also knew I was alone at my apartment, so he immediately asked if there was some place I could go and be around friends. I stood up from the middle of my living room floor and told him I could go back to my friends' apartment that I had just left 15 minutes earlier. Granddad made me promise him that I wouldn't stay at the apartment by myself. I assured him I was getting ready to drive back to my friends' place, and before we said our goodbyes he told me he would be in Bloomington the next morning to pick me up and bring me home.

I hung up the phone and just sat on the floor for a good while. All I really wanted to do was start driving home, but Granddad didn't want me to do that by myself. I knew I needed to stay in Bloomington and wait for him to arrive. He had said several times on the phone that he didn't want me to be alone, that I needed to go somewhere away from my empty apartment. When I needed help the most, it was his voice that was there for me to hear, and follow.

Since it was past midnight and David, Brandon, and Ted had all been heading to bed when I left their place, I wondered if they would even still be up. I didn't call over there before I left my apartment. I couldn't. I wasn't in the mood to break the news or talk to anyone or really even be around anyone, but I had made that promise to Granddad: I would find company. I wouldn't be alone.

I figured I would take a quick drive back over there, see that their apartment was as quiet as all the other units in their complex had been when I left there not long before, and then turn around and come back to my apartment. That way I could at least tell Granddad I tried to go over there, but I didn't stay because I didn't want to wake up the whole apartment.

What I found when I got back to my friends' apartment complex was not what I was expecting at all. Thinking back on that moment still gives me chills to this day. Less than an hour ago, their apartment complex was so vacant and quiet you could have heard a raindrop hit the pavement. When I got back over there this time, however, the parking lot in front of their apartment was almost full. All their lights were on, the door was open, and there were a number of my friends and teammates already waiting inside and outside the apartment. Of course much of the campus had already emptied out as people headed home for summer break, including many of those associated with the basketball program. Since I hadn't called anyone, I'm still not certain how anyone found out what had happened, or how they knew that I would be coming back to BDT's. But there they all were, including some close friends of mine that weren't connected to the basketball program. A passerby would have thought some sort of party was underway, maybe celebrating the final day of school. I got out of my car and . . . now I just remember snapshots from what took place over the next few hours.

At about 1:30 AM, our assistant coaches, John Treloar, Mike Davis, and Pat Knight, came to see me at the apartment. I walked outside and talked with them for an extended period of time. They told me they had just heard the news and hadn't been able to get in touch with Coach Knight yet, which was understandable considering how late it was. I hope they realize how much it meant to me that they took the time to come out and check on me.

I remember sitting on the couch at BDT's, waiting for any kind of call with information on what was going on back home (the storms had knocked out a lot of the phone service in my home area in Tennessee). We just kept watching the same ESPN SportsCenter highlights over and over again. Mainly, we talked as much sports as we could, just to push through the awkward silences that arise in a time of sorrow.

I remember that while some of us were in the middle of some random sports conversation in the living room, I could hear someone crying from another area of the apartment. This led Brandon to ask someone who was heading in the direction of the crying, "Could you tell [the person crying] to keep it down a little?" These were two incredible gestures of friendship. For a friend to be so overcome with emotion for me that they were brought to tears said a lot about the closeness of our friendship. At the same time, Brandon's sensitivity in trying his best to get my mind off the situation for just a little while and shield me from additional sadness showed a level of compassion anyone would like to have in their friendships.

Mainly I was trying to piece together what had just happened back home. I still didn't have a lot of the details on how the tragedy had occurred. It helped just to talk to someone for a few moments about the what-ifs, could-haves, and should-haves that everyone goes through at a moment like that. I really don't remember if I went back to my apartment or if I stayed at BDT's all night. I don't even remember if I slept or not. My memories pick back up the next morning when my granddad and two close family friends came by to pick me up. The 350-mile ride back to Lobelville were filled with their words of encouragement, some of my words of anger, and words of prayer by all of us.

I hadn't been home in Tennessee for very long, maybe ten minutes, when a group of people knocked on the door. It was Coach Knight and all of the assistant coaches. By the time Coach Knight heard the news about my mom that morning, we were already on the road back to Tennessee. Coach Knight had immediately set up a flight on IU's private jet so that he and the coaching staff could get to Tennessee as quickly as possible to pay their respects. I'll never forget that gesture. Their tremendous support truly lifted my spirits, and it amazed me they would come that quickly to show how much they cared about me and my family.

Coach Knight put his arm around me and asked if there was a place we could sit down and talk privately for a while. He and I walked into the empty kitchen and sat down at the table, the table at which my mom and I had shared hundreds of moments, from blowing out birthday candles to working on school projects. What I remember most about what he said to me was about my mom having raised me and provided for me as a single parent on a teacher's salary. He told me I was going to go through some tough times, but he knew I could handle it because of how my mom had raised me. Coach Knight leaned toward me in his chair and said, "*I know you have that kind of toughness in you, because your mom had that kind of toughness in her.*"

After Coach Knight and the staff headed back to Bloomington, my granddad and I went to visit the site where the tornado had hit and taken the lives of both Mom and Hollis Hinson. Since returning home I had learned that in many ways our
county had been really fortunate. There had been three fatalities
caused by the violent F4 tornado (207 to 260 miles an hour)
that had touched down in Linden: Mom, Hollis, and a fourteen-
year-old girl named Brandi Mathis. But it easily could have been
much worse. The tornado came close to hitting dozens of other
homes, but fortunately steered clear of them.

When we arrived at the site, I noticed that Mom's white Nis-
san Maxima was still parked in the exact place in the driveway
where she had left it the night before. The same car that she had
taken on countless trips to Bloomington was still parked just
fifteen feet away from the rubble that remained of the house's
entrance.

The strength and precision of the tornado was gut-wrench-
ing to think about. Hollis's relatively new house was completely
obliterated. There was nothing but inches of rubble and debris
left where a house had stood just twenty-four hours earlier. Yet
my mom's car had been completely undisturbed, sitting there in
pristine condition. If Mom and Hollis had defied all logic and
warnings and had decided to wait out the storm in her car, they
would have had an inexplicably safe front-row seat to watch the
destruction that took place in just a matter of seconds.

The debris field extended a couple hundred yards into a
wooded area behind what was left of the house's original foundation. My granddad and I walked over the area, helping some of
Hollis's family look for any possessions and personal effects that
might be salvageable. As I was walking along the debris field, I
came upon an item that made my heart sink: what was left of
the bathtub that my mom had gotten into while seeking shelter
in the bathroom. That meant that this was the exact spot where
they had found my mom, about 100 yards from the house.

One of the things I realized after you lose someone close to you is that your life becomes full of firsts:

> *The first time I picked up my phone and began to call my mom before I realized she wasn't going to be there to answer anymore.*

> *The first morning I woke up at our home and forgot for a few early-morning moments that I was now alone in the house.*

> *The first Thanksgiving and the first Christmas without Mom, who was always the anchor of our holiday get-togethers.*

I had to wait a while for many of these firsts to come around eventually, but one that I didn't have to wait too long for was my first Mother's Day without a mom. Her funeral was on Saturday, May 8, and Mother's Day was that Sunday. My granddad—remarkably—was able to go ahead and preach the Mother's Day sermon that he had prepared well before he knew he would be delivering it the day after his daughter's funeral.

I don't remember much about what Granddad said in that sermon, but I do remember he said this about my mom:

> "She was a jewel."

Two Tickets to Utah

Coach Knight knew it was going to be important for me to stay busy the rest of that summer in 1999. So he figured the best way to keep me busy and my mind occupied with basketball was to send me on some serious road trips. The rest of my summer included extended stays in Madison, Wisconsin, Salt Lake City, Utah, and Vienna, Austria. The trips to Wisconsin and Austria were both tied to the Big Ten All-Star tour that our conference sponsored that summer. Players from every team in the Big Ten went to practice for a week in Madison with our head coach for the tour, Wisconsin coach Dick Bennett. After a week of practice we traveled to Vienna for a couple of weeks to play various European teams. I had never thought I would be so happy to find a McDonald's, but after about three straight days of eating wiener schnitzel in Austria, an order of Chicken McNuggets sounded as good to me as a New York strip. As incredible an experience as the overseas trip turned out to be, it was the trip to Salt Lake City that would lead to an unlikely acquaintance and a moment that left me speechless.

Coach Knight had coaching friends across the country and across a vast array of sports. One such pal was Rick Majerus, then head basketball coach at the University of Utah. One of the kindest things that Coach Knight did for me in the months after my mom died was to get me in as a counselor for Coach Majerus's basketball camp. Now, if it had just been me going off to Utah alone for a week to be around a bunch of people I didn't know in a place I had never been, I would not have been that thrilled, but Coach Knight suggested that my granddad should go with me, which meant the world to both him and me. If there was ever a time we needed to take a trip together thousands of miles away from home, this was definitely it. It said a lot about Coach Knight. He wasn't just concerned about me coping with the loss of the only parent I had ever really known, but he was also concerned about my granddad coping with losing his only child at the young age of forty-seven. So off my granddad and I went to Rick Majerus's Utah Utes basketball camp.

From the very first day as a counselor for Coach Majerus, I was impressed with how hands-on he was with all the drill work that the campers were going through each day. I have been to various college coaches' camps, clinics, and so on, and the typical approach is for these head coaches to let their counselors (usually the host team's own players) and their assistant coaches

Knight Lines

Mental is to physical as 4 is to 1.

—Coach Knight

Junior year, 12/1999

run a lot of the drills and day-to-day operations. Coach Majerus's approach was not like that at all. He was right in the middle of all the drills, yelling, encouraging, and teaching the youngsters as they worked on various types of skill improvement drills. Much of how Coach Majerus directed traffic on the basketball court with his booming voice (and creative language) reminded me a lot of how Coach Knight ran things on the court. It was easy to see why these two guys got along. At the end of each session Coach Majerus was in need of a new shirt because within the first half-hour of the first session his was already saturated with sweat.

I actually didn't talk with Coach Majerus much for the first few days of the camp. On the first day, he made sure to come over and talk to Granddad and me, but it wasn't a conversation that went into any depth. It was basically just a "glad you guys could come out this week" kind of chat. He did mention to us that in the evenings the counselors would play pickup games on the Huntsman Center court after the camp had ended. On one of the last nights of the camp, the pickup games were especially memorable. That night Andre Miller, a former Ute who had been the no. 8 pick in that year's NBA draft, showed up to play a couple of hours with all the counselors. Luckily for me, he and I ended up on the same team that night, and we went on a nice run of wins during the course of the evening. I had been used to being around some pretty good passers at Indiana, especially guys like Michael Lewis and Tom Coverdale. But Andre Miller was a rare talent, with a gift for seeing the court and delivering passes exactly where they needed to be at the exact time they needed to be there. That night was the best I played while I was in Utah. After all, I was on the floor with a guy who would lead the NBA in assists just three years later.

The night before our last day of camp, Coach Majerus made a point to come over and have a brief chat with Granddad and me. He went over some things he liked about my game and some things that he told me I needed to improve on. Then, the last thing he said to me that final evening in Utah was this: "Make sure you guys find me after the camp is over tomorrow." I told him we would, and with that Granddad and I headed back to our hotel for our last night in Salt Lake City.

The next day the camp wrapped up around noon, and all the campers were shooting a few more shots on the court before they left for home with their parents. Amid the flurry of activity on the court at the conclusion of the camp, Coach Majerus motioned for me and Granddad to follow him down a long hallway just off the main court. The three of us walked several feet back into this hallway, far enough that the commotion on the court could barely be heard. Coach Majerus didn't say anything to either one of us until he had come to a complete stop. This conversation would end up being just about as brief as the other two we had had with him that week, but from the tone of his voice I could tell that there was going to be something different about this one.

"Kirk," Coach Majerus began, "I know you've been through a terrible tragedy, losing your mother. When I was younger, I went through a tough time after a loss of my own. I was fortunate to have some people around me in my life that did a lot to help me out during that time. And because of that I've always tried to help out kids that I know are going through a real tough time."

At that moment Coach Majerus reached into his pocket and brought out a white envelope and handed it to us. He continued: "I hope this helps you all out. I'd appreciate it if you don't tell anyone about that [he pointed to the envelope] and if anyone ever asks me about that, I'll say I don't know anything about it."

Granddad and I had been standing in our footprints since the first words had come out of Coach Majerus's mouth. We both were so shocked by his words and gesture that we had barely drawn a breath in the past minute, much less said a word. I finally mustered a thank-you, and Granddad and I both added that he didn't have to give us anything. We were just glad to come out and be a part of the camp and the pickup games. But Majerus insisted we keep the envelope as he began to walk with us back to the basketball court. We didn't even know what was in the envelope; we hadn't looked in it yet, but as we were leaving Granddad directed one final comment to the thoughtful Utah basketball coach: "All of this was awfully kind of you."

With that, Granddad and I headed up the long set of stairs leading to the arena's exit. As we walked out of the arena and began to head to the airport, Granddad and I looked into the envelope that Coach Majerus had given us and in it we found. . .

. . . Sorry, Coach Majerus *did* ask us not to tell.

12

An Intolerable Policy?

What exactly was the infamous zero-tolerance policy that garnered so much attention during Coach Knight's final year at Indiana? That's a question that many, even those who lived through the fiasco that was Coach Knight's dismissal, still have a difficult time answering even today. Perhaps with the help of some of the exact language that was in the zero-tolerance policy, we can once and for all understand what this policy was all about as it pertained to Coach Knight at Indiana in 2000:

> Public presentations and other occasions during which coach Knight is a representative of Indiana University will be conducted with the appropriate decorum and civility. Included among these occasions are interactions with the news media. Failure to do so will be cause for further sanction, up to and including termination from the position of basketball coach. A task force will be established to develop policies for appropriate behavior for all coaches, athletic department employees and

162

student athletes, and for sanctions for not following these policies. The task force will make its recommendations on these policies to the athletics committee, the president and the board of trustees. ("Indiana Keeps Coach Knight with Sanctions"; see bibliography)

Well, I may have been wrong about this information helping us understand the policy better, because after reading it I think I'm now more confused than ever! So, the zero-tolerance policy was a policy that created a policy-creating task force that could create more policies? That sounds more like the plot of an awful *Twilight Zone* episode than it does a plan to keep an athletic department running smoothly.

OK, so let's see if I can describe this in as simple terms as possible.

The zero-tolerance policy was put into effect specifically for Coach Knight by then Indiana University president Myles Brand and the IU Board of Trustees in May 2000. This was largely in reaction to a basketball practice video that was leaked to CNN a month earlier, a video that may or may not have stemmed from Coach Knight trying to make a call on what he thought was an open line. Instead, the line was in use, allegedly with an assistant coach (not so wisely) criticizing Coach Knight harshly, which may or may not have led to an assistant coaching vacancy, which may or may not have led to the infamous Neil Reed tape being leaked to CNN in 2000 that showed Coach Knight using his right hand to stop Reed dead in his tracks in the middle of a practice.

"Nothing this strongly and systematically has ever been done before" was how President Brand described the zero-tolerance policy. A more apt way of portraying it, though, would be this: "Nothing this broad and so conveniently and easily enforceable has ever been done before." However you decide to describe the policy, one thing is for certain. It would eventually lead to one of the darkest days in Hoosier basketball history—the end of the Knight era at Indiana.

The policy's objective, according to Brand, was to act as both "a series of sanctions and one last chance" for Coach Knight. What it seemed to some of us on the team, however, was a policy designed to make it possible to fire Coach Knight at a more opportune time than the summer of 2000 would have been. If Coach had been fired when the policy was implemented, it would have given my teammates and me ample time and opportunity to transfer to other programs had we chosen to do so. Transferring in the middle of a semester, however, just before the start of the basketball season, is a much tougher decision to pull the trigger on—and I'd have a hard time being convinced that Brand and the Board of Trustees didn't let this factor into how they set up and implemented their zero-tolerance policy. The zero-tolerance policy was a perfectly designed "parachute policy" that could have its rip cord pulled anytime Brand chose to tug.

For the team, it was three months and twenty-three days of basketball business as usual in Bloomington after the policy was first announced—and then three days of dealing with

Knight Lines

If you don't aim the gun at the duck and look at the duck . . . then the duck s _ _ _ s on your head.

—Coach Knight

Sophomore year, 11/17/98

an overdramatized reaction to an interaction that never really warranted Coach Knight's dismissal. On Thursday, September 7, 2000, a nineteen-year-old IU freshman, Kent Harvey, walked past Coach Knight in Assembly Hall and said to him, "Hey, what's up, Knight?" Coach Knight put his hand on "the inside of his elbow" in an effort to correct the kid, telling him that he should address him as "Coach Knight or Mr. Knight" (Belmont; see bibliography). Even Harvey himself thought the interaction was a nonissue. Years later he recalled, "I learned a story can get sensationalized. . . . The encounter with Bob Knight and me was over-emotionalized" (Rabjohns; see bibliography).

I have to say that I am somewhat apprehensive about delving into this topic, because so much of it revolves around Myles Brand, who in 2002 became president of the NCAA and who is now deceased. I don't enjoy speaking out against the actions of a person who has no chance to defend his position. However, the tipping point for me came when I read the transcripts from Brand's press conferences in May and September 2000 in regard to the implementation and execution of the zero-tolerance policy.

Brand portrayed the zero-tolerance policy as having "very specific, very firm guidelines," but on further review "inconsistent" would be a better description. From my perspective, many things that transpired the week of Coach Knight's firing were disappointing, not just the part that made the headlines. Near the top of my list was our team meeting with Brand, which took place in our locker room, sans Coach Knight, on Saturday, September 9, 2000, one day before Brand's televised announcement that Coach was being fired. Brand began our meeting by making some brief remarks about the process that had been taking place concerning Coach Knight's job status, while noticeably dancing around the main topic—never flatly saying whether or not Coach Knight had been fired. He finished talking to us and then opened the floor for questions. It was well known among us that he had met with the Board of Trustees the day before, so the point-blank question that one of the players directed at Brand that evening was this:

What did you and the IU Board of Trustees decide at yesterday's meeting?

President Brand did his best political tap-dance routine to avoid being pinned down by a bunch of 18–22 year olds with a question he didn't want to answer. In the same room where Coach Knight would meet with us just twenty-four hours later for the final time, Brand answered, "No final decision has been made yet." My teammates and I had many questions about the validity of the policy and its enforcement, but President Brand offered us very few satisfying answers that night.

On Sunday at his press conference, Brand officially announced that Coach Knight had been fired while continuing the politician polka he had performed for us at our meeting the day before.

> **Reporter:** *Had a decision been made [about Coach Knight's firing] before your meeting with the players on Saturday?*
>
> **Myles Brand:** *At that point I was getting the evidence from the IU Police Department. I think the facts of the matter are clear, even if not every interview had taken place. With my conversation with Bob Knight this morning, we reached the point that we should go forward now.*
> ("Indiana University Basketball Coach Bob Knight Fired"; see bibliography)

Another of Brand's remarks that never made a lot of sense to me had to do with timing—the choice to enforce the policy in September.

> **Reporter:** *What was it that broke the camel's back, if there was such an event?*

Myles Brand: *There really wasn't such an event.*
What we had was a pattern of activity. . . .
Unfortunately there has [sic] been many instances in
the last seventeen weeks in which Coach Knight has
behaved and acted in a way that is both defiant
and hostile.

So "there really wasn't such an event" (according to Brand) "that broke the camel's back," but there was a "pattern" and "many instances in the last seventeen weeks" that necessitated the removal of Coach Knight? This is one reason why I believe "inconsistent" is a fitting adjective for the zero-tolerance policy—especially if you take into account what the initial stipulations were when it was first implemented four months earlier on May 15, 2000:

Myles Brand: <u>*Any failure*</u> *on Coach Knight's part*
to meet these standards will be cause for further
sanctions up to and including termination of his
position as head coach of Indiana University's
basketball team.

It's a zero-tolerance policy. Nothing this strongly
and systematically has ever been done before.
("Indiana Keeps Coach Knight with Sanctions"; see
bibliography)

If it truly had been a "zero-tolerance policy," wouldn't that have meant that one of the "many instances" over the previous seventeen weeks should have triggered additional sanctions or the immediate termination of Coach Knight? If there had been "many instances," why were there no more sanctions levied, and why wasn't Coach Knight fired at a date that wasn't so close to the start of basketball season? I think it wasn't in the best interests of the powers-that-be to pull the ripcord on the policy

too soon—if they had, they would have found their top reve-
nue-producing athletic program in total disarray as player after
player transferred out of town. Perhaps Brand also realized that
the policy's stipulations were too strict and that it would be absurd to suspend, fine, or fire a legend like Coach Knight because
of incidents such as the one when he sternly instructed an administrator to leave the gym after she interrupted a practice and
randomly began talking to one of the assistant coaches. (Coach
Knight himself intimated that he didn't think the decision to fire
him was made that weekend in September. At his campus farewell address to over 6,000 Indiana students at Dunn Meadow,
Coach Knight said, "This [firing], believe me, had happened to
me long before" ["Knight Says Goodbye to IU, Students"; see
bibliography].)

On Sunday evening, September 10, Coach Knight met with
his Hoosier team in Assembly Hall for the last time. We had
gotten word from trainer Tim Garl that Coach Knight wanted
to meet with all of us in the locker room, the same room where
Coach Knight had taught lesson after lesson about how to play
the game of basketball for almost thirty years. It was in this locker room that he prepared his players to compete against teams
coached by men named Boeheim, Henson, Pitino, and Krzyzewski. But now, Coach Knight was facing an opponent that didn't
have a sharp-shooting guard or a shot-blocking post player for
him to devise a successful game plan against. Instead, he was
facing a policy that seemed to have been devised to be unbeat-
able—and conveniently enforceable.

The Assembly Hall entrance had been inundated with reporters the past several days, with the number of news trucks in the
parking lot peaking the night of our final meeting with Coach
Knight. Afterward, my teammates and I filed out of Assembly
Hall and waded through the reporters and their questions as we
headed back to our apartments to contemplate our college basketball futures. I remember Suzanne Malveaux, a reporter from

NBC (now with CNN), asking me that week about my thoughts on President Brand firing Coach Knight. Letting my affinity for movies come into play, I told her Oliver Stone could do his next JFK-like conspiracy movie in Bloomington and entitle it *RMK*. There was a lot that didn't feel quite right to me about the process and the decision back in 2000, and I feel the same way today.

The final team meeting with Coach Knight—about ten hours after the announcement of his firing—was ultra-emotional, for all involved. It was difficult for our team to come to terms with the fact that Coach Knight was no longer our head coach. This was tougher than any loss we had experienced playing for the Hoosiers. Our basketball family was going to be incomplete. Dane Fife said it well: "It was tough to deal with because our team, our family, was being broken apart" (Leung; see bibliography). Coach Knight told us he hated the fact that he "wasn't going to have a chance to coach this team because I think this team could do something special." We were all so proud to be a part of the Hoosier basketball tradition that Coach Knight had raised to such heights at Indiana University.

Dane Fife described the situation pretty well. Coach Knight, he said, "saw the hurt in us. He saw Odle and he saw Haston. Haston who had been through hell the previous summer. I think he realized how much he meant to us, and that was special for us to know that. It was sad, and yet it was a unique and special moment, too. It was just a moment that you don't get with Coach Knight very often" (Hutchens; see bibliography).

Whatever the case may or may not have been, the disdain the team felt toward the zero-tolerance policy was palpable. In the days following Coach Knight's firing, players were filled with frustration because of the decision's flimsy reasoning and the forced timing of the policy's enforcement. What we wanted was to be led by Coach Knight in Assembly Hall, but what we got was a policy that led to Coach Knight being forced out of Bloomington.

Imagine If

After LeBron James and the Cleveland Cavaliers lost to the Golden State Warriors in the 2015 NBA Finals, Nike creatively spun LeBron's saga into a popular "Imagine if" advertisement. Here are just a few lines:

> *Imagine if LeBron came home to Cleveland.*
>
> *Imagine if they faced the top seed in the Finals.*
>
> *Imagine if everyone counted them out.*
>
> *Imagine if they defied odds, logic and the basketball gods to come back and win the series in 7.*
>
> *Except this isn't Hollywood. It's Cleveland.*
>
> *Nothing is given. Everything is earned.*

This is similar to the way I look back today on what could have been if Coach Knight had remained the coach of the Hoosiers. It crushes me that Hoosier fans never got a chance to see what plans Coach Knight had in store for our team in the 2000–2001 season—and that my teammates and I never had a chance to be part of those plans.

The final preseason workouts we had under Coach Knight allowed us a glimpse into some of the plans he had for his post players. He had placed me, Jared Jeffries, Jeff Newton, and George Leach in the same individual workouts. Coach Knight was envisioning stretches in games when all four of us would be on the court at the same time—6'9", 6'11", 6'9", 6'11". Coach had noticed my improved range during shooting drills, and he came over to me while I was shooting three-pointers one day and simply said, "*You need to be ready to step out and hit threes this season.*" Jeffries also had good range as a shooter; he and Newton were both exceptional for big men when it came to ball handling and driving to the basket. What Coach Knight

Knight Lines

I'll coach the offense and the defense, but
I'll be d_ _ ned if I have to coach effort.

—Coach Knight

Junior year, 3/7/00

was seeing in those September workouts, when only four players could be coached at a time, was something visionary and
radical. He felt that most of the Big Ten was trending toward a
small-ball style, away from big, traditional post players, which
to him meant a lot of the teams would be vulnerable to a big-
man attack. He was working toward a surprise that I guarantee
no one would have seen coming: a zone defense. That's right,
Mr. Man-to-Man Defense himself was working on the idea of
throwing a 1–3–1 Knight-zone at teams for a few minutes each
game—a *big* 1–3–1. His idea was to put the athletic 6'11" George
Leach and his pterodactyl-like wingspan at the top of the zone
to hound the opponents' point guards and then just let the trap-
ping chaos ensue.

Unfortunately, none of us got the chance to play for Coach Knight
that season, and none of Hoosier Nation got the chance to watch
this plan in action. But just imagine what could have happened. . .

*Imagine if the zero-tolerance policy had never been
implemented.*

Imagine if Coach Knight had never been forced to leave IU.

Imagine if Coach Knight had retired as an Indiana Hoosier.

Except this isn't Hollywood. It's Bloomington.

13

Friendship Tolerance

When I think back of all my time with Coach Knight, a lot of moments come to mind, but one of the coolest took place on January 20, 1999. Coach Knight had requested that Dane Fife and I come over to his office (aka "the cave") on the lower level of Assembly Hall. It was about as different a setting as you could imagine compared to the brightly lit, well-furnished office he used upstairs in Assembly Hall. Just a few days earlier, we won a double-digit victory at Purdue, but we had learned in the past that a good victory didn't automatically provide a safe haven from criticism.

As Dane and I headed for our meeting with Coach Knight, we knew that there was a good chance that we would be spending the next few minutes going over our mistakes from the Purdue game and Coach's corrections. Dane and I walked into the office and shut the door behind us. I noticed Coach was in the middle of watching game film and thought to myself, "Yep, we are definitely in for a film session showcasing our mental errors from the Purdue game."

It was just Dane, me, and Coach Knight in the room. Coach fiddled with the remote in his hand, pausing the game film he had just been watching, then didn't waste any further time getting to the point of this meeting. *"You both are smart kids, but you both have to be smarter on the court. Kirk, you don't need any more talent than what you've got, but you have to play tougher. Boys, you two are the hub of this team in the future."*

And with that, the meeting was over, and Coach sent us on our way with a new responsibility on our shoulders, but one that we were honored to have.

Dane was a sarcastic, hardworking competitor who to this day has probably never met an argument he didn't think he could win. He was also "that guy" who you never wanted to play *against*, but always wanted to play *with*. We had our share of heated moments on the basketball court as we competed against each other. As a matter of fact, we really got into it after a (typical) hard foul he made on me in a pickup game one day in Assembly Hall. After the play, while I held the basketball, we jawed back and forth. Then, from about fifteen feet away, I threw the ball as hard as I could at him.

Unfortunately, I missed him—he ducked out the way by shifting to his left (no wonder my pitching career amounted to nothing in high school). Then my misguided leather missile headed right for the player standing a few feet behind Dane, our 6' 11" center, George Leach. The basketball hit him right in the family jewels, sending him down to one knee as he writhed in pain and moaned, "What did *I* do?!" It was typical of Dane to come out of that kind of battle unscathed. He had a knack for pushing all the right buttons on an opponent, getting the riled reaction he wanted and then getting away with it while all the while having a "Who . . . me?" look on his face. There were very few, if any, players I would rather go into a Big Ten battle with than Dane Fife. But after Coach Knight was fired, it looked like there was going to be very little chance of us being teammates again.

Knight Lines

Kirk, if I had a daughter I'd want you to date her.
I'd say three things to you and have you so
f _ _ _ ing scared that you wouldn't even hold
her hand and you'd have her back thirty minutes
before curfew . . . I wouldn't let her date Dane.

—Coach Knight

Sophomore year, 1/20/99

Dane was passionate about playing for Coach Knight, and now he seemed equally passionate about his distaste for the how, why, and when associated with Coach Knight's removal as our coach. The entire situation had Dane ready to transfer as soon as possible, and I couldn't blame him. Several players had similar feelings and were also seriously contemplating transferring, including me, but since I had already gone through one year of sitting out because of my redshirt season, I really had no interest in sitting out another year if I to transferred to another school.

However, the distinct possibility that many of my teammates might be transferring made me realize that leaving the program might not be that dumb an idea if there would be few, if any, Big Ten–caliber players left on the team over the next two seasons (especially the season that was about to start).

In the immediate aftermath of Coach Knight's firing, the team felt disjointed. Like a fighter who had just gotten his bell rung and needed some time in his corner to get the ringing out of his ears, most of the players on the team went back to their rooms and tried to collect themselves and think about what their next moves should be. I remember going to Dane's apartment two or three evenings in a row for some impromptu team meetings to discuss if we were all going to stay or go our separate ways. I pleaded with my teammates who were thinking of transferring to stay so we could show everyone what the team Coach Knight had brought together was capable of achieving. Dane, however, was so mad about the situation that he was adamant about transferring. I don't know how much time and how many conversations Dane and I had about our team's situation, but I tried to get my points across to him about keeping the team together in those days immediately after Coach Knight's firing. I wanted him to hear my pitch on why he should stay as often as I could get him to listen, if for no other reason than just to keep the thought of transferring from filling up his mind completely. I was incredibly relieved when Dane told me he was going to stay at Indiana. I think things would have been drastically different (and not for the better) for most of us on the team if he had not chosen to stay and help keep Coach Knight's team together.

It took several meetings at Assembly Hall with the Athletic Department brass to make sure that all the players would stay in Bloomington. We probably could have gotten a business course credit on our transcript for the negotiation lessons we learned. Time after time, we would sit at the large conference room table with the Athletic Department suits and talk about how we all could make the best out of this mess of a situation. We were resolute about not wanting an outsider to be hired at such a late stage. We were just weeks away from the first game, so we felt the smoothest transition was for one of the current assistant coaches, Mike Davis or John Treloar, to be named as the interim head coach. None of us was interested in trying to adjust to an entirely new coaching staff, so we made sure to let the athletic director, Clarence Doninger, know that if Indiana University wanted to keep the entire roster of players in Bloomington, we needed to have either Davis or Treloar named as our head coach for the 2000–2001 season. We got our wish—actually, our demand—when Mike Davis was named the interim head coach of the Hoosiers.

All this eventually led to a 21-win team, a Big Ten Tournament Championship game appearance, and a no. 4 seed in the NCAA Tournament in 2001. It led me to making the Associated Press All-America team, which would have been an impossibility if all my teammates hadn't stayed at Indiana. And last but definitely not least, keeping the team together in 2001 resulted in Fife, Jeffries, Odle, Coverdale, Hornsby, Newton, Moye, and Leach earning a much deserved Big Ten title for IU in 2002, along with making the Final Four that year and ending the season as the national runner-up in the championship game. Those guys are a part of Indiana basketball history in a way that I had dreamed of being but was never able to achieve. Their 2002 team owns a legacy you can't attach a value to.

In the days following Coach Knight's firing I told Dane, "You need to stay here because we still have a lot we can accomplish." This was similar to what Dane said to me a year later when he wanted me to come back as a fifth-year senior instead of entering the NBA draft. When I made my pitch to Dane to stay, he trusted what I said and ultimately chose to stay at Indiana. I know that Dane had to feel somewhat betrayed when I chose not to return to the Hoosiers' team for the 2001–02 season. It was difficult to hear Dane give me the same pitch to stay that I had given him while at the same time knowing that what was best for me was to declare for the NBA draft. I completely understand why he felt that I was letting him and the team down. It was fitting somehow that we both ended up trying to convince the other to stay at the school that Coach Knight brought us to. One friend listened and took the advice, and one friend listened and didn't. To this day, it still bothers me that in my situation I didn't think it was in my best interests to stay, even though I would have been returning the favor and repaying Dane for the loyalty and trust he had shown to me.

Dane has never let me off the hook for leaving IU in 2001, even years later. Before Dane was an assistant coach at Michigan State, he was the head coach of the Mastodons of Indiana University-Purdue University-Fort Wayne (IPFW). It 2007 I finally had a chance to see and talk with Dane for the first time in six years. My wife, Kasey, and I drove up to Indiana to watch his Mastodons play the New Jersey Institute of Technology Highlanders (which ended up a 52–47 victory for his Mastodons). The morning of the game I drove over to the IPFW basketball offices for a visit. It took all of two minutes after I walked into his office for him to say, "It was a dumba-s decision for you to not come back and play with us in 2002."

Just like old times.

After we visited for a few more minutes there, he invited me to go down to the Mastodons' practice facility to play some morning pickup games with him and his assistant coaches. After Dane and I made sure that we weren't on the same teams, the games began. Over the next couple of hours, Dane hit me with a few elbow shots to the ribs and I hit a few sky hook shots over him.

Just like old times.

(Except this time, I didn't throw a ball at Dane's head and accidentally hit one of the other players in the "mastodons.")

Sky Hook Meets Air Jordan

It was four days after Christmas in 2001 when our Charlotte Hornets team bus arrived at the MCI Center (now called the Verizon Center) in Washington, D.C., for a matchup against the Washington Wizards. A year earlier this game would have barely been a blip on the sports radar in Washington. But this game, like all the other home games for the Wizards that season, was sold out. Over 20,000 fans packed the arena to watch their team's president of basketball operations, Michael Jeffrey Jordan, take the court as his NBA un-retirement tour rolled along.

Jordan's return to basketball at the age of thirty-eight had been a success up to that point in the season. He had the Wizards above .500 and was averaging 20 points, 5 rebounds, and 5 assists per game—great numbers for any player, but quite remarkable for someone that age who had thousands of playing miles on his odometer. It was fair to say, however, that his performances up to this point had more of an NBA journeyman feel to them rather than the iconic superstar vibe MJ had exuded for so many years. Some of the guys on the team even joked that Jordan was no longer "Air Jordan" but "Floor Jordan." However, on this December night in D.C., it would be His Airness that would get the last laugh.

Knight Lines

I knew you didn't have the f_ _ _ ing balls
to do that! Cheaney didn't and f_ _ _ ing
Michael Jordan didn't, so I know you don't!

**—Coach Knight
(said with a smirky grin—I promise)**

*Freshman year, 2/1998, when Mike Lewis decided
to pretend he was going to walk out and skip Coach's
film session and leave the locker room, but quickly turned
around and came back in (Jordan, by the way, played for
Coach Knight on the 1984 U.S. Olympics squad)*

As warm-ups began I kept sneaking peeks at the other end of the court, watching the Wizards go through their layup lines. I kept trying to time my trips to the back of our layup line with Jordan's so I could jog right past him near the half-court line. It was absolutely blowing my mind that I was just a few feet away on the same court with the man whose highlight videos I had watched countless times when I was just a kid in Lobelville. The first time I actually saw Michael Jordan in person was at a minor league baseball game in 1994 when my mom had taken me to see MJ and his Birmingham Barons play against the Nashville Express during his first retirement from basketball. I was fifteen years old and was standing next to the dugout with a *Sports Illustrated* and a Sharpie when Jordan first emerged from the dugout steps. Seven years later I was getting set to (hopefully) play in the same NBA game against him in my first season in the league. Warm-ups ended and I looked around at the 20,000-plus fans sitting in the stands. "Nobody has a better seat for this Jordan game than me," I thought to myself.

It didn't take long to realize that something special was going on that evening. After the first quarter, Jordan had 24 points, a new Washington franchise record, beating out Bernard King's 23 in 1990. Jordan cooled down somewhat and scored only 10 points in the second quarter, but that was still enough to set the franchise record for points in a half, barely nipping Jeff Malone's previous record of 33 in 1988. At halftime it wouldn't have shocked me if one of the Hornets' team administrators had pulled me aside and told me that I was going to be fined for my semi-celebrations on the bench as Jordan poured in jumper after jumper over the outstretched hands of our own defenders.

Before it was all said and done, Michael Jordan and I had combined for 53 points in the game. Jordan *did* have 51 of those points, but he missed 17 shots in the process, while on the other hand I was 1-for-1 from the field on a nifty little sky hook I made from the right block just in front of the Wizards bench. It was a sight to behold in person. OK, not my perfectly swished hook shot, but Jordan's dazzling performance. I would have been thrilled if I had been in the stands and been able to say to my kids that I was in the arena for a Michael Jordan 50-point game. I never thought I would one day look back at my basketball playing days and fondly remember a game that my team lost and in which I scored just two points. But to have been on the team that it happened against and to have actually gotten to play in the game that Jordan scored 51 points has made it a very cool memory.

After the game, as we were getting dressed and ready to head to our team bus, a Wizards ball boy came into our locker room. The ball boy had a large pair of sneakers in his hands, and by the look on his face you could tell he was looking for one of the Hornet players. As luck would have it, the ball boy was looking for longtime NBA veteran Stacey Augmon, who was sitting in the locker stall directly across from me. This gave me the chance to hear what the ball boy told Stacey, or "Ice," as most people on the team called him. The ball boy handed Stacey what looked like a brand new pair of white and blue sneakers and said, "Mr. Jordan has been signing his game-worn shoes after each game and giving them to a player on the opposing team that he really respects. He told me to make sure that I got these to you."

I hope that Stacey didn't think I was staring at him as he got dressed. I really was just staring at the size 16, one-game used, Nike Air Jordan sneakers that MJ had just scored 51 points in and that also just so happened to have a HUGE "Michael Jordan" signature on the side of each of the shoes! I'm a sports collector nerd, so I can't help it. I've gotten excited over pulling an Antawn Jamison autograph out of a pack of basketball cards before. So it wasn't any surprise at all that I was blown away by this authentic piece of Michael Jordan memorabilia sitting across the way from me. I was finally dressed and began to head out the door to the bus. As I walked by Stacey's locker he causally picked up Jordan's very own Air Jordans and said, "Hey, Rook, would you carry these to the bus for me?" As I made the long walk toward the team bus, I felt like I needed white gloves and an armed guard to escort me the rest of the way.

14

Number 1 Comes to Town

The 2000–2001 basketball season was my junior year of playing basketball for the Hoosiers and my senior year in the classroom. Seeing the man you came to play basketball for canned as your head coach is about as far removed as one could imagine from how you would like to start your fourth year as a college basketball player. But this is exactly the position that my teammates and I found ourselves in as the 2000–2001 season approached. The decision had been made to name one of our assistant coaches, Mike Davis, as the interim head coach. Naming either Coach Davis or the other assistant, John Treloar, to be the new head coach was probably the only move the athletic director could have made if the school wanted to ensure that all the players Coach Knight recruited to IU remained Hoosiers.

Our 2000–2001 season started off a little bit shaky. We did get two wins to start the season, versus Pepperdine and South Alabama. However, we promptly lost three games in a row with lackluster performances against Temple, Texas, and Indiana State. By the time the Big Ten portion of our schedule rolled around, we were beginning to play somewhat better, but we

Knight Lines

Boys, I want you to walk off the court with others saying, "Man, I wish we could play like that."

—Coach Knight

Freshman year, 11/29/97

were still nowhere near the level of play that had gotten us into the Top 10 in the AP polls in each of the previous two seasons with Coach Knight.

We battled back to a 9–5 record heading into our first Big Ten conference game at Wisconsin on January 4. We gave the Badgers everything they could handle, but in the end we got drawn into playing the typical grind-it-out, Wisconsin-style game and lost 49–46. This dropped us to 9–6 heading into our Big Ten home opener versus the defending NCAA champions, the Michigan State Spartans. Michigan State was rolling into Bloomington on a twenty-four-game winning streak (dating back to the end of the previous season) and was the no. 1 ranked team in the nation at the time. The game was the first sellout at Assembly Hall since Coach Knight's dismissal, with over 17,000 fans packed in to watch the nationally televised Sunday afternoon game. The game was physical throughout. By halftime, we had shoved and elbowed our way to a 28–27 lead. The second half was more of the same, a typical rough-and-tumble Big Ten matchup. Neither team could pull away from the other. As we entered the final three minutes of the second half, it seemed that whoever had the ball last was probably going to control their own fate.

Freshman Jared Jeffries, the hometown Bloomington stand-out, played an outstanding game on both ends of the floor that afternoon. Jared and I ended up doing the most damage for our team on the offensive end; he and I were the only Hoosiers to reach double digits, scoring 16 and 27 points, respectively, in what was a relatively low-scoring game. We found ourselves with the ball, trailing 57–56, with only twenty seconds remaining, but we missed an opportunity to take the lead after I missed a good look from around the foul line and MSU's Jason Richardson was fouled in the scrum while going for the rebound. So with 12 seconds left on the clock, Richardson had a 1-and-1 at the free throw line and a chance to make it a 3-point game.

Richardson missed the front end of the 1-and-1, but at about the same time the Hoosier faithful in Assembly Hall was reacting with loud cheers at his miss, they started to gasp because MSU's Zach Randolph had just done what he does best: work hard to position his body into perfect position to grab an offensive rebound. The Assembly Hall cheers over the Richardson miss quickly faded into moans as Randolph was fouled going back up with the rebound he had just muscled down. As he headed to the line with 11 seconds remaining to shoot two, it seemed we had perhaps just blown our chance to upset the no. 1 team in the country.

Randolph, 2 for 2 in the game from the foul line before this point, missed the first but made the second shot to give MSU a 58–56 lead. Tom Coverdale then hurried with the in-bounds pass to mid-court and called a timeout with 8 seconds left on the clock. In the huddle Coach Davis set our strategy. We weren't going to try to tie the game and send it into overtime. The play called for our best three-point shooter, Kyle Hornsby, to get the ball near the top of the key. If he had the open shot, great, but if he didn't, we hoped the action of the play would draw enough attention from the Michigan State defenders that I would be open on the right wing as I popped out after setting a down-screen for Hornsby. Down two points, we wanted to live or die with a three-point shot and, if all went right, give the defending NCAA champions their first loss in twenty-four games while at the same time jumpstart our own season.

The inbounds pass went to Coverdale, who dribbled it to the left wing while Jared Jeffries and I set a staggered double-screen for Hornsby to send him to the top of the key. As the top man in the staggered screen, I could immediately pop back behind the three-point line for a pass from Kyle. Randolph was guarding me, and we thought he might switch off to Hornsby, leaving the shorter Charlie Bell to have to switch and guard me—or, if we were lucky, we might end up with both Randolph and Bell chasing Hornsby, leaving me wide open. But MSU's Tom Izzo is an elite basketball coach for a reason: his team played perfect defense. Randolph extended just far enough off my screen to allow Bell enough time to recover and guard Hornsby. Bell did even better, flying around our screens so quickly that it forced Kyle to catch the ball ten feet behind the three-point line, guarded tightly by Bell. And Randolph recovered back to the wing to guard me. Hornsby caught Coverdale's pass, pivoted in my direction, and passed me the ball with 3.5 seconds remaining. Randolph was crowding my right side so much that I couldn't just catch and shoot, so with 2.3 seconds on the clock, I put the ball on the floor for one bounce and escape-dribbled to the left to create just enough space away from Randolph to get a shot off from behind the arc with 1.5 seconds left on the clock.

As I released the shot, I slowly started to backpedal toward the half-court line. I don't remember hearing a single sound in the gym as the ball was in the air.

As soon as that ball went through the net, the deafening cheers of 17,000-plus Hoosier fans hit me in an avalanche of sound. I remember turning to the scoreboard above the visitors' team basket on the other end of the court and seeing all zeros on the clock, then turning back around and seeing Tom Coverdale's no. 3 jersey closing in on me. He tackled me to the floor, with Kyle Hornsby, Jarrod Odle, Andre Owens, and hundreds of court-storming students piling on soon thereafter.

I quickly found myself on my back on the court with several dozen people on top of me. It was an odd feeling to experience the explosive loudness of Assembly Hall at the exact time that everything around me in the gym was almost pitch black because of the cascade of people over me. My legs were completely pinned to the floor, and no matter what I tried to do to get up, I couldn't free myself from the mosh pit that was now the area just in front of the MSU bench. I was just about to the point where I was getting a bit worried about the position I was in when I saw something that reminded me of Andre the Giant back in the old WWF Royal Rumble days. In much the same way Andre would enter the ring of a Royal Rumble match and just start throwing guys like Hacksaw Jim Duggan, Koko B. Ware, and Big Boss Man out of the ring, Tom Coverdale was now literally tossing random undergrads left and right off the pile until he could give me a hand to pull me up.

I had no idea at that moment, but it was history: the first time IU had ever beaten a no. 1-ranked team at Assembly Hall.

The first game-winning shot I had ever tried was the one I missed at the buzzer in the state championship game my junior year in high school in 1996. Now, five years later, I was successful on my second try. This time the feeling was indeed a lot different, but ironically, I ended up doing the exact same thing in the locker room in Assembly Hall that I had done in the locker room after that state championship loss in 1996. After Coverdale helped me up off the court, I somehow made it back into our locker room before anyone else. I was just there alone; my ears were ringing from the noise that was still sounding on the other side of our locker room wall out on the court. I sat down on the floor, put my arms on my knees, dropped my head, and thought about how much this moment would have meant to my mom.

The first time I had ever cried after a basketball game was because of a lost game and a missed shot. The second time I ever cried after a basketball game was because of a made shot and a missed mom.

Knight Lines

It doesn't take many f_ _ k-ups in life to ruin it.

—Coach Knight

Junior year, 12/25/99 (Merry Christmas!)

Breakfast Invitation

Our team was in Orlando, Florida, for the NCAA Tournament in March 1999. The morning after our first-round victory over George Washington, Coach Knight had a 10 AM practice scheduled, which meant our team bus would be picking us up in front of our hotel at about 9:00. A few teammates and I had finished our breakfast early, so we went outside to wait for the bus. After being cooped up indoors for several months of a Midwest winter, it was a refreshing change of scenery to be down in Florida for a few days.

Tom Geyer, Luke Jimenez, and I were standing outside near the hotel's entrance, just outside the shade of the large, covered portico where hotel guests were being dropped off and picked up. We still had about fifteen minutes until the bus would arrive, so while we were all waiting there, I decided to use this opportunity to entertain my teammates with my latest Coach

Knight impression. It wasn't that doing impressions was a talent of mine; almost everyone on our team, for better or for worse, had his own Coach Knight impression (which could probably be said about *every* Bob Knight team, anywhere!).

Anyhow, I launched into my very own Coach Knight tirade impression that I had been honing for over a year: "KIDS TODAY JUST AREN'T FOCUSED ON WHAT'S IMPORTANT, THEY WANNA DUNK AND THROW BEHIND-THE-BACK PASSES INSTEAD OF SETTING UP CUTS AND SETTING SCREENS!!" My impression sounded like a cross between Christian Bale's Batman and Tom Izzo after three straight Big Ten tourney games. It wasn't a great impression, but it was good enough under the circumstances to get a few chuckles from my small audience. Just as I was basking in the glow of my successful rendition of a Coach Knight speech, I heard a vastly different reaction—not at all like the chuckles I had just heard from my teammates. It was a booming voice coming from right above and behind me that gruffly barked, "HASTON!" down in my direction. Either someone else was doing an incredibly accurate Coach Knight impression of their own . . . OR . . . and this was the possibility that I knew, unfortunately, was the correct one. Coach Knight himself was some way, somehow nearby. I froze in my tracks for a moment, as if by simply standing completely still I would be less visible to Coach Knight, wherever he was.

I pivoted around from the pillar of the hotel portico where I had been standing and looked up. Coach Knight was leaning over the edge of the railing, enjoying a doughnut and staring a hole straight through me. The top of the hotel's portico just so happened to also serve as the deck of Coach Knight's hotel suite (information that would have been nice to know about three minutes earlier). Coach Knight had been there the whole time and heard every word I had just uttered. The next thing that happened was a first for me. Coach Knight invited me to breakfast.

*"Haston, would you like one of these doughnuts . . .
maybe fill up that mouth of yours so you can't talk as much?"*

15

Day Camp and Knight Chats

*I*n my final season at IU, we finished in third place in the Big 10 with a record of 10–6, which included wins in seven of our last nine games. We then won two games in the Big Ten Tournament, losing only in the championship game to Iowa. With that resume we earned a no. 4 seeding in the NCAA tournament and a first-round matchup against the no. 13 seed, the Kent State Golden Flashes, in San Diego, California. I was eager to get back onto the court for March Madness so I could get the bad taste out of my mouth from our first-round loss to Pepperdine the previous year. I had missed all but the first four minutes of the contest after I tore a meniscus and strained the lateral collateral ligament in my right knee in a collision with a Pepperdine player.

At halftime against Kent State we led 42–34, and we were feeling pretty upbeat heading into the locker room. That mood would be in stark contrast, however, to how we felt the next time we set foot in that same room a little more than an hour later. The second half was pretty much all downhill. This turn of events could be attributed mostly to the outstanding play of Kent State's

6'1" junior guard, Trevor Huffman. Huffman had been good for most of the contest, but in the last five minutes of the game he came through with a couple of critical (I would say borderline incredible) shots that put the game out of reach for us. Huffman ended up scoring 24 points as he propelled his Golden Flashes to the kind of first-round upset that NCAA tournament junkies love. After the game Huffman said that the Indiana guards were strong and physical, far more than he was used to playing in the Mid-American Conference, but that "quickness-wise, that [advantage] belonged to us" (Ewell; see bibliography). Another setback we ran into in the second half was that our primary ball handler, Tom Coverdale, was hampered by a hip injury and then fouled out on a ticky-tack reach-in foul. After the game Coach Davis elaborated on the problem this situation caused our team: "I don't want to make any excuses, but Tom Coverdale is the only point guard we have. Without him we started panicking and didn't hit guys that were open" ("Indiana vs. Kent State"; see bibliography). Coverdale's limited minutes along with the fact that both Dane Fife and Jared Jeffries were also in foul trouble in the second half created a perfect storm that we just couldn't overcome. We did get a great spark off the bench from A. J. Moye, who gave one of his best efforts of the season and just when we needed it most. But he and I were the only Hoosiers to reach double digits, scoring 29 and 12 points, respectively, not enough to help us overcome Huffman's play and our own late turnovers. Once again, our season ended earlier than it should have.

Final score: Kent State 77, Indiana 73.

After we returned to Bloomington from San Diego, I spent the next couple of months finishing my classes and contemplating the opportunities in front of me. If I stayed in school, I was going to have an incredible group of teammates to play with in an attempt to finally win a Big Ten championship and make a deep run in the NCAA tourney. But the NBA was a serious possibility for me, and that was weighing heavily on my mind. So without committing either way, I decided to accept an invitation to the NBA pre-draft combine at the Moody Bible Institute in Chicago in June. This would allow me to go through the combine and play in games against other potential draftees in front of NBA scouts from all thirty teams. Since I had chosen not to sign with an agent, I was not risking any college eligibility under NCAA rules, and at the end of the camp I could still get a better idea of how high I might be drafted if I decided to declare for the NBA.

To say that the NBA pre-draft combine is a stressful experience is a major understatement. It's especially tough when you're a big man who has to rely on guards to pass you the ball when their own self-interest is tied up in shooting as much as possible in order to impress the NBA scouts. In the end, however, I came out of the camp looking like one of the few forwards who could consistently hit a jump shot. ESPN's Andy Katz called the overall shooting at the camp "awful," but he had this positive note to add: "Haston's consistent mid-range 5/8 [FG/FGA] and 6/12 performances . . . might have pushed him into the late first round and away from Indiana."

My first couple of days at the combine went well and led to some unusual interactions with a variety of NBA franchises back at the hotel where all the participants were staying. Most of the meetings I had were very secretive, usually arranged by someone sliding an envelope under the door at some random hour, with a letter inside giving you the number of a hotel room and an exact time to be there. Sometimes the letter didn't even identify the team. In one meeting, almost the entire brass of an NBA franchise was packed into a regular-sized hotel room. They directed me to a seat next to the window near the edge of the room and then asked me a series of questions: about my general thoughts on the game of basketball, how I approached playing board games, and more. The most in-depth interview I had was with an East Coast team (not the Charlotte Hornets); at the conclusion of that interview, someone handed me a bubble answer sheet and a multiple-choice test booklet and asked if I would be willing to take a twenty-page test before I left the meeting. I gladly sat down with my #2 pencil, read the questions, and filled in the bubble answer sheet the best I could for the next hour.

Overall the camp went about as well as I could have hoped. If I had stunk up the joint, then maybe my decision to stay in school would have been made for me. But since it didn't play out like that, I headed back to Bloomington knowing that declaring for the 2001 NBA draft was a real option for me. I wasn't sure what my final decision would be. In the days following my return to campus in Bloomington I would go back and forth several times on whether or not I should stay for one more season or declare for the NBA draft.

This was a big change in my thinking from the previous year. At that time—the end of my second year playing for Coach Knight—the possibility of playing in the NBA never crossed my mind, even though that year had been a breakout season for me (15 points and 8 rebounds a game). Sure, like anyone else playing D1 basketball, I held onto a long-distance hope that my childhood NBA dream could come true someday, but it was just floating around the back of my mind, nothing close to realistic. That's why I was surprised when Coach Knight asked me before that 2000–2001 season began:

> *Are you going to come back to school after this next season or are you going to leave?*

I honestly had no clue what he was talking about, so I hid my ignorance by just shrugging my shoulders and keeping my mouth shut. As soon as I got back to my apartment, I wrote in my journal the exact thought that went through my head when

he asked his question: "Leave for what?" The thought of entering
IU for the NBA draft had never entered my mind, but months
before I had played a single game of my junior year, Coach
Knight was already projecting that I would have the type of season that would put me on the radar of NBA scouts.

The pre-draft combine was almost nine months after that talk
with Coach Knight, and I hadn't seen or talked to him even once
during the 2000–2001 season. As a matter of fact, I didn't talk to
him for the rest of that school year. It was in June when I decided
I would break the silence and reach out to Coach Knight, who
was still living in Bloomington. I was in dire need of guidance
and wanted to ask someone with valuable experience about my
NBA decision. The draft deadline was fast approaching, and so
with only a short period of time left to make a huge decision, I
dialed Coach Knight's home number. As his phone continued to
ring, I was just hoping he would pick up and share a few words
of wisdom with me, maybe a four- or five- minute conversation
with some classic life advice from Coach Knight. What I got instead was completely unexpected: "*Kirk, why don't you just come
on out to the house and we'll talk about your options.*"

Coach Knight's and Ms. Karen's house was in a residential
area that looked like your typical all-American neighborhood. If
you had expected that the Knights would be living in some large,
private compound with pit bulls and military-grade surveillance
cameras around every corner, you would have been surprised.
Their house had a long tree-lined driveway, which gave their
house a private feel by the time you reached their front porch. I
got out of my car and knocked on the front door of their large
cabin-like home. Coach Knight quickly answered and had me
follow him through their living room, where I noticed there
were quite a few moving boxes strewn about, a reminder that
Coach would soon begin his tenure as the head coach of the
Texas Tech Red Raiders in Lubbock, Texas. I also noticed a huge
bookcase in the living room lined with history books and books

about the military. There was little doubt in my mind that the books weren't just there for display purposes, but that Coach Knight had studied them as thoroughly as he studied game film.

We continued to the back of the house and into a large, screened-in porch area and took a seat in what seemed to be Coach Knight's version of a man cave. Judging just by all the trees in the backyard, it was hard to believe we were only a pitching wedge away from a handful of nearby houses. As I looked around, I saw several more moving boxes on the floor, but there were still plenty of cool items on display. One that drew my attention was a picture from a fishing trip of Coach Knight and his good friend Ted Williams, the all-time baseball great. Next to the picture was a fishing hat that Williams had given Coach Knight. Coach noticed me looking in the direction of the picture and hat, which also had a number of fishing flies attached to it. *"Those fishing flies were actually tied by Ted Williams. It really says something about a man when he becomes an expert in one field, and then when he's done with that he becomes an expert in something entirely different. Ted Williams became the best hitter in baseball and then went on to become one of the best fishermen in the world."*

At this point, I really was more interested in hearing Ted Williams stories, but then Coach Knight started talking about the reason I had come to see him. We talked for ten minutes about basketball and my future, and then somehow we got off onto another topic altogether—maybe golf for fifteen minutes—before getting back to discussing college versus the NBA. Coach mentioned several NBA contacts he had and said he would be glad to give them a call and find out what the teams, scouts, and other experts were saying about my potential draft position. This offer just backed up what Coach Knight had always told his players from the first day they set foot on IU's campus: *"I'll always be there to help the guys who played for me and graduated."*

OK, I hadn't quite yet gotten my degree, but I guess Coach felt

I was close enough to my graduation date to go ahead and give me a hand in gathering information for this major life decision I had in front of me. That night we swapped stories and talked about some memorable games as well as some close calls that made us sick to even think about. It was such an extraordinary experience to be able to sit and talk with Coach Knight one on one and pick his brain about basketball, baseball, golf, and history. This was especially true considering that it had been just eight months since he was forced out at IU and I wondered if I would ever have the chance to see or talk with him again. Over the course of the next seven days Coach invited me back out to his house four more times. At the end of the week I weighed all the pros and cons of staying in school and leaving for the NBA, and finally focused on three factors that all leaned in the direction of declaring for the draft:

> A) I was healthy.
>
> B) I was coming off a season in which I was named to the AP All-America team.
>
> C) I had had a successful NBA pre-draft camp.

It's tough enough as a college basketball player to have even two of these factors lined up in your favor, much less all three. Based on the above factors as well as a few others, I was considered a potential first-round draft pick. This was an opportunity that not too many 6'9" small-town white guys with a twenty-eight-inch vertical leap ever have, and probably should not let pass by. In my heart I wanted to stay in Bloomington and play with a college team that I loved to play for, but in my mind I knew it was the right time to make the jump.

I've heard quite a bit of speculation over the years about how Coach Knight tried to sabotage Coach Davis and the Indiana basketball program. Even Coach Davis himself has said he had heard the rumors, including about Coach Knight convincing me to declare for the NBA draft ("Ron Felling vs. Bob Knight";

see bibliography). But these are the facts. First, I already had my own opinion about playing another season for Coach Davis, so it really wouldn't have mattered what Coach Knight had said to me about him anyhow (which, by the way, was nothing as far as I can remember). Second, Coach Knight never once approached me to volunteer any type of advice during or after the 2000–2001 basketball season. He certainly didn't seek me out at the conclusion of the season in an effort to tell me to leave school for the NBA draft. It was only after *I* called *him* and asked if he would use some of his NBA connections to look into my draft potential that he ever discussed anything with me about my immediate basketball future. As a matter of fact, the last piece of advice he gave me before that first phone call I made to him in June was the same advice he gave to all of my teammates in the locker room during our final team meeting with him: "*You're at a great university. You have a great chance to be an outstanding team. Stay together and do the best you can. I'm only sorry that I can't coach you because I know that's why most of you came here, and I think we'd have a great team.*" Four days later he echoed some of the same sentiments in his farewell address to over 6,000 students at Dunn Meadow: "*When you go into Assembly Hall for the first game this year, I want you to remember what your moms and dads, your brothers and sisters, your aunts and uncles and friends that have been in those seats before you have meant to our basketball team. And I want you to mean the same thing to this basketball team.*"

That sure doesn't sound like a man who would try to sabotage the Indiana Hoosiers basketball program.

Life after Knight

Over the first five games of the 2000–2001 season, I was the team's leading scorer and rebounder. I suffered a sprained toe and missed one game (the only game I ever missed as a Hoosier due to injury). It was a very minor injury, but it was December and everyone involved decided it was best for me to rest for one game so it wouldn't be an issue once we got into Big Ten conference action. By the next game I was fully healthy and ready to play. Coach Davis didn't start me that first game back, which I thought was understandable. I found it less understandable, however, when he didn't put me back in the starting lineup for the next four games, even as I was coming off the bench and still leading the team in scoring and rebounding.

Here were the numbers. I had averaged 30 minutes, 18 points, and 10 rebounds per game in the first five games of the season. Then, after missing one game and losing my starting job, my playing time dropped over the next five contests to 24 minutes per game and my season averages dropped to 15 points and 9 rebounds. It may have been easier to understand the situation if Coach Davis had come to me and explained why I had lost my starting job and what I needed to do to earn it back, but he never did. Although I had started the first two games of our conference schedule (Wisconsin and Michigan State), it wasn't until I hit the game-winning shot versus the top-ranked Spartans that I felt confident I had truly worked myself back into the starting lineup for the rest of the season. And in fact I did start every game following that shot. I definitely wouldn't say I had a bad relationship with Coach Davis; I appreciated his taking the interim head coaching job because it kept the team together that season. In my time with him I found him to be very personable and thoughtful and easy to get along with, but I concluded after my benching that his level of confidence in my game wasn't very high. Maybe it was because I wasn't one of the players he recruited; maybe he just didn't think I fit the style of basketball he wanted to play. Whatever the case, it had become obvious to me after that five-game stint coming off the bench that I didn't have a wide margin for error in Coach Davis's eyes. So when I was weighing whether to turn pro or return for the 2001–02 season, that realization made me question whether I wanted to entrust my future basketball options to a coach who I suspected did not value my abilities all that highly. I had a lot of positives lined up in my favor at the end of my junior year, positives that I didn't know would all be there again if I chose to come back and play as a fifth-year senior.

Spending time with Coach Knight as I was contemplating whether to stay or go was one of my favorite weeks I spent at IU. However, it was sad to think that it would turn out to be one of the last weeks that he and I could both call Bloomington home. The time passed quickly on the night of my last visit to the Knights' home. It hadn't seemed like I had been there very long, but as I stood up to leave, I realized we had been talking for well over an hour. It also didn't seem that long ago that Coach Knight had asked if I wanted to play for him at Indiana. It didn't seem that long ago when Coach, his assistants, and my teammates traveled down to Tennessee to be there for me when I lost my mom. And it didn't seem that long ago that he told my teammates and me after a Big Ten victory that he was *proud of the way you boys competed.*

Drafty Reception

There were three moments in my post-college basketball career that will forever stand out in my mind—for all the wrong reasons. Many athletes and coaches will tell you that they have a much more vivid memory of their "bad beats" than they do of their great accomplishments. That's definitely the case with the following three stories. The first is from the night after I was drafted by the Charlotte Hornets, the next is from my rookie season, and the final story is from my NBA Developmental League days.

The toughest decision I had to make while at Indiana was to

Knight Lines

Kirk, have you ever read the first chapter
of Genesis, verse 5?
You should go read it—it says,
"Thou shalt see both sides of the court."

—Coach Knight

Junior year, 2/11/00

forgo my final year of eligibility and declare for the NBA draft. As fate would have it, I would make this decision just months before my Hoosier teammates would win a Big Ten title and advance all the way to the 2002 NCAA championship game versus the Maryland Terrapins. My choice to leave for the NBA and my subsequent absence from a memorable Hoosiers basketball team has been frequently pointed out to me in articles, blog posts, and Twitter messages over the years (along with "friendly" jabs from Dane Fife while playing golf). I even had to endure some ribbing from Tony Kornheiser and Michael Wilbon on ESPN's *Pardon the Interruption* during one of their head-on-a-stick segments. There's nothing quite as stomach-churning as seeing the name "HASTON" on the PTI rundown board when you know you haven't done anything good lately. (Seeing that, I was hoping there was maybe some obscure golfer named Chuck Haston who had come out of nowhere to shoot a 59 in a tournament that day.) Even my hometown isn't safe. There is nothing like your golfing pals bringing up things like missing out on a Final Four run just before you stand over a crucial putt (yeah, I'm talking about you,

Caleb Dunkle, Eric Lomax, Barry Cunningham, Brent Hinson, Trent Hill, and Aaron Foster . . . not that I'm keeping up with that sort of thing). It's amazing the strange paths of embarrassment that can result from one decision in your life—as when someone points out to me, years after the fact, that I was selected in the draft before . . . wait for it . . . six-time NBA all-star **TONY PARKER!!!** That's right, Tony *flippin'* Parker was taken after me with the twenty-eighth pick in the 2001 draft. You want to talk about major ghosts-of-close-calls past, look no farther than all the teams that passed on Tony Parker before that twenty-eighth pick. I'm sure a lot of NBA general managers still have nightmares about not drafting Parker before the San Antonio Spurs nabbed him late in the first round. Don't get me wrong—I'll always appreciate the Hornets for drafting me (I'm guessing the feeling is not mutual), and I'll be glad to see them succeed in the future, but leaving Tony Parker on the board in 2001 has to sting a bit (pun intended).

I'll never forget the day after the draft. I came back to Bloomington, and I went straight to the School of Health, Physical Education & Recreation (HPER) field house where the annual Hoosiers' Basketball Camp was in session on all ten of its basketball courts. I couldn't wait to see my (now former) teammates one last time before I headed to Charlotte. I walked in wearing my new Charlotte Hornets draft cap and saw everyone stationed at their assigned courts, running camp drills. As I made my way through the camp, my former IU teammates were far from rude. Most gave me a quick congrats before quickly continuing their drills. But I slowly realized that I had completely misjudged what sort of greeting I would get in returning to Bloomington. Maybe I was just so excited about getting drafted, but in my mind these guys were still my teammates and I thought they would be excited too when I came back. And I think that would have been the case—if I hadn't left one year of eligibility on the table. That fact made my return to campus feel a bit icy. This was painful to realize, especially in the middle of my little return tour.

My brand new, purple and teal Charlotte Hornets cap and I made our way to an upstairs court where Jarrod Odle was leading some drills. To his credit, Jarrod had some very kind things to say. Maybe he was just happy to have a significant amount of playing time open up due to my departure, maybe he was really happy for me, or maybe (and probably) it was a little bit of both. Nevertheless, I appreciated what he had to say that evening. And then, looking back a year later, the fact that he took that opportunity for increased minutes and converted it into a successful senior year made me feel a trace better about the whole visit.

I made my way back down the corridor of steps leading to the main gymnasium area, where I would have to go past all my former teammates and relive my walk of shame one more time. As I walked down the stairs and approached the HPER courts filled with my former teammates and their campers once again, I took my Charlotte Hornets cap off, folded it up, pushed it deep into the back pocket of my jeans, walked as fast as I could toward the door I came in, and left for Charlotte, North Carolina.

A Burger with a Side of Sighs

Another close-call memory of mine occurred in 2002 because, as fate would have it, I found myself back in the state of Indiana just in time for the Hoosiers' to play their Elite Eight game in front of 22,435 fans in Rupp Arena in Lexington, Kentucky. My Hornets teammates and I arrived in Indianapolis the day before our game against the Pacers—which also just so happened to be the day the Hoosiers were going for a little revenge against the team that had knocked IU out of the tournament the previous season, the Kent State Golden Flashes. This was IU's deepest run in the NCAA tournament since an Elite Eight matchup versus Kansas in 1993. The showdown against Kent State was a game that I could have been playing in, but on this memorable Indiana basketball night I was watching the game with my Hornets teammate Bryce Drew at an Applebee's in Indianapolis. The atmosphere in the restaurant was probably just a *tad* different from what my former Hoosier teammates were experiencing as they took the court.

It didn't take me long to realize that I wasn't going to have much of an appetite during this game, and that I probably would have been better off just sitting in my hotel room by myself. If it hadn't been for Bryce being there, I probably would have exited stage-left well before our waitress had even refilled my sweet tea the first time. There are only so many finger-pointings, stares, and comments like "Don't you wish you had stayed one more year, Haston?!" that a person can handle in one night—and I reached my max pretty quickly that evening. It absolutely wrecked me not to be a part of that Hoosier team. To not be able to play for my school, in that atmosphere, for those types of stakes, with that group of players was a soul-crushing experience. The Hoosiers, of course, went on to defeat Kent State 81–69 and advance to the Final Four for the first time since 1992. I can only imagine what the celebration must have been like for my friends after that game.

The next day I was walking into the visitors' locker room at Conseco Fieldhouse (now the Bankers Life Fieldhouse) after the Hornets' 99–84 win over the Indiana Pacers. It was a game in which I didn't play a single minute. Yet I found myself surrounded by multiple news cameras and reporters as I sat down at my locker in my bone-dry no. 35 Charlotte Hornets jersey. It seemed like the questions from the Indiana-based reporters were coming at me in rapid-fire succession:

"Did you watch the Hoosiers' Elite Eight game last night?"

"How did it feel to watch your former teammates celebrate their Final Four berth?"

"Kirk, can you tell us if you wished you'd stayed one more year at IU?"

"What would you like to say to your friends who are on their way to play for a national championship?"

It was embarrassing to be the one talking to reporters and staring into TV cameras while guys sitting next to me who had actually just played in the game, like Jamal Mashburn, Baron Davis, and P. J. Brown, barely had any reporters hovering around them. The whole experience over those two days back in Indiana reminded me of a line from the movie *Tin Cup*. Kevin Costner's character, Roy McAvoy, has just shot an awful first-round score of 83 at the U.S. Open, and his caddy, Romeo (Cheech Marin), offers these words of "comfort" for his golfing pal: "You're humble now, homes."

Trolled by Sager?

It's obviously not a fun transition to go from the lifestyle of the NBA to life in the D-League. The differences are night and day. In the NBA we traveled on a private team plane, which not only had extra-large recliner seats for each of the players, but also a staff that would have your favorite large Pizza Hut pizza and favorite drink (mine being an "Arnold Palmer," sweet tea plus lemonade) ready and waiting for you when you boarded the plane after road games. In contrast, in the D-League you would pile into your bus and ready yourself for an eight-hour ride to Huntsville, Alabama, that would include exactly one break, at a Pilot truck stop, where your meals usually included some combination of a Slim Jim, Doritos, a honey bun, and a flat 44-ounce Pepsi. It can happen just like that in professional basketball. One second you're in the NBA staying at Ritz Carlton Hotels from Miami to L.A., and the next minute you're sitting on a twin bed in a random Ramada Inn somewhere, listening to the streaming audio of a D-League draft on your laptop and waiting to find out that with the fifth pick a team called the Florida Flame has selected you to play for them.

However, there was some good news in my deportation to the D-League, and that was who my new head coach was going to be down in Fort Myers, Florida. My three-year contract with the Hornets was behind me and it was time to move forward and try to earn another NBA opportunity. It was exciting to find out that I was going to be playing for three-time NBA champion Dennis Johnson, who most basketball fans simply referred to as "DJ." I would have given a good chunk of my NBA rookie paycheck if I could have had Dennis Johnson as my head coach with the Hornets. He had that same "I trust you enough to give you a chance" quality that I had experienced playing for Coach Knight.

After one of our first practices Coach Johnson told me to "be ready for us to come to you." His encouraging words were the most positive push I had had since college. It was largely because he was my head coach that I had a successful season in the D-League. His belief in me brought back the confident feeling that I had had much of my time at Indiana but that had been drained out of me during my seasons with the Hornets. During my season in Florida, Coach Johnson helped me realize that if I played like I was capable of playing there was a great possibility that I would get that NBA call-up I so desperately wanted.

Thanks in large part to Coach Johnson's confidence in me and the opportunity he provided, I bounced back from two dreadful years with the Hornets to average 16 points and 8 rebounds a game and earn the "honor" of making the All-NBA D-League First Team. It's always nice to be recognized for your effort, but when you're in the minors you really hope you aren't there long enough to earn too much recognition for being there.

Finally, late in the season, Coach Johnson's belief in me seemed to have finally paid off in the biggest way possible—almost.

After one of our final home games in Fort Myers, I was told that Craig Sager (yes, that Craig Sager, of colorful-coat TNT fame) was outside our locker room and wanted to talk to me. I had been told he had a home in the Fort Myers area and just liked coming to nearby Estero, Florida, to watch basketball even when he wasn't working games. I had never met Mr. Sager before, although I had seen him dozens and dozens of times on TV working the sidelines of various NBA games over the years. I had had a pretty good game that night, so I figured he just wanted to tell me "nice game" and then ask a question or two about playing for Coach Knight (which happened a lot, by the way). As I exited our locker room (actually a locker room for a minor league hockey team, the Florida Everblades), Sager came right over to me, and I could tell he was eager to tell me something.

Mr. Sager pulled me over to the side of the hallway and said, "Kirk, I talked to a scout that was here tonight, and I wanted to give you the news first. You are getting ready to be called up." I . . . was . . . beside . . . myself with excitement. I couldn't contain my smile as I managed to reply with a stammering "Really?"

"Yes," he replied. "If I were you I'd go wait by my phone."

I headed out to my vehicle, checking my cell phone for calls and voicemails every step of the way. As thrilled as I was, I felt more relief than anything that I was going to get a second chance to prove myself in the NBA. All the hours spent working out in random gyms and all those night bus rides had paid off. I was going to be putting on an NBA uniform again. And this time, hopefully, I would show all the people who had made fun of me and called me a failure and a flop that I could play in the NBA. I felt ready to take advantage of this opportunity. It was just a few months ago that I thought I had lost my game completely, but now thanks to Coach Johnson I had confidence that I was now ready for this second chance at the NBA.

I called my granddad and told him I should be getting some big news soon about a call-up and that I would phone him back when I knew what NBA team I would be flying out to join. But when I got to my cell phone, there were no voicemails and no missed calls. I just sat in my SUV in the parking lot for about forty-five minutes, waiting and waiting for that phone call that could change *everything* for me. But that call never came and I never played in another NBA game.

I know, I know—my story isn't quite in the territory of an Archie "Moonlight" Graham from *Field of Dreams*, but I can definitely relate to the what-if misery old Doc Graham must have felt. I never found out what happened that night. Maybe the scout was talking a little above his pay grade to Sager or perhaps the team's GM decided not to follow the scout's recommendation—or perhaps Craig Sager is the most ruthless and diabolical practical joker of all time!

To this day, when Sager pops up on my TV screen I can't help but let out a Seinfeld-esque "SAGER!" in that "NEWMAN!" kind of way.

16

Image Is Something,
but Not Everything

*I*t will come as no surprise that when Coach Knight was upset, he was going to let you know why he was upset and what you should do in order to fix what had made him upset. His tough demeanor always kept his players on their toes, but what would really catch us off guard when he was trying to get a point across was not his temper but his humor (most of it intentional, some not so much). Even at his angriest he could very quickly, and unexpectedly, switch to humor, and then, if he wanted, just as quickly revert to anger again.

October 18, 1997

Coach has just noticed on the game film that A. J. Guyton has bent over, grabbed his shorts, and taken a quick rest while play on the court was still live. Coach rewinds and pauses the video right at the point where A. J. is bent over and tugging on his shorts. "*A. J., what are you doing here? What are you in position to do, A. J.? You are in perfect farting position. A. J., are you fart-*

ing here?" [Coach stands up and mimics A. J.'s bent-over position that's now frozen on the screen behind him in the locker room.] *"Because if you're farting, you're in great position. You're not in position to do much else, but you sure can fart in this position."* [Coach now stands back up.] *"You know, A. J., some of the greatest farters started in this position before moving on to bigger and better farting positions."*

December 1997

Starting point guard Michael Lewis made a comment to the team at the beginning of practice that Coach Knight agreed with—but then Coach paused for a long time and stared at Lewis the way someone might stare at a painting while pondering the real meaning of the piece in front of him. After a few seconds of silence in the gym, Coach Knight grinned and said, *"I had to*

Knight Lines

You guys don't realize who you are playing for. You're playing for more than just yourselves. You're playing for people all around the state. You're playing for fans, for kids that are sick, for little old ladies that can't get out of the house. For two hours the other night you caused a lot of enjoyment.

—Coach Knight

Junior year, 12/25/99
(four days after Indiana defeated no. 8 North Carolina)

think for a second, Mike. I'm always so f_ _ _ ing mad at you, I wasn't sure if I still was today."

January 1998

At the conclusion of a very subpar practice, after which we were supposed to go eat supper and come back to watch game film at 7 PM, Coach Knight summed up our effort for the day with the following speech:

> *Everything has to be comfortable for you guys! Just go ahead and leave and do whatever. Go out with your girlfriends, do whatever . . . I know you think I'm full of b_ _ _ s_ _ t, well I think you're full of b_ _ _ s_ _ t too! There, now we both think we're full of b_ _ _ s_ _ t! Go ahead and leave and come in for pregame tomorrow if you want to, and then come to the game if you want to, whatever's comfortable! Just don't come back here [tonight]! I won't be here and there will be NO coaches here!*

After Coach left the locker room, we all decided that it would still be wise for us to show up at Assembly Hall for the scheduled 7 PM film session. I had eaten a late lunch, so I skipped supper and decided to kill time by getting in a few shots before the meeting. It was just ten minutes after he had basically told us not to bother to come back for the meeting, but Coach came out of his office, walked over to the goal where I was shooting, and for the next twenty to thirty minutes, in as calm and patient a manner as you can imagine, worked with me on my shooting technique and fed me pass after pass from the wing down into the low post.

I saw Coach Knight lose his temper plenty of times, but what may surprise people is that he was often not nearly as angry as he seemed. Coach would cleverly put on the "General's Cap" from time to time just to get a point across to one of his players,

Knight Lines

Haston, I'll f_ _ _ing quit the day when
I don't think I can make you a tougher player.

—Coach Knight

Junior year, 12/1/99

or he would go on a tirade just to get into the heads of the referees, and also (though this is strictly my suspicion) to give the fans a little of what they bought a ticket to see.

I'll never forget the time we were in a heated Big Ten battle in Assembly Hall when a ref's call didn't go our way. Coach called a timeout. As we were heading off the court to our bench, Coach Knight let this referee know the displeasure he felt over the call just made. This was done much to the delight of the 17,000-plus fans in Assembly Hall that day. He proceeded to walk alongside the ref and have a one-way discussion with him for a solid fifteen seconds as he made his way to our bench. To all in attendance and anyone watching the game on TV at home, it would have looked like he had surely lost his temper and was totally incensed. But once Coach Knight got back to the bench, he took his seat in front of us and with a hint of amusement calmly said, *"That son of a b_ _ _ h never has liked me. Now, boys, this is the play we're going to run when we go back out there."*

February 5, 1999

Just because we had won our last game versus Wisconsin definitely didn't mean that any of us were safe from scrutiny when it came time to have our play evaluated on the big projection screen in our locker room. When Coach Knight has the remote in one hand and a laser pointer in the other, everyone is fair game on the game film—especially a certain 6'9" sophomore forward who had struggled mightily right off the bat in that last contest. I was so awful early on that Coach Knight pulled me out within the first minute! That's right—I started the game and was benched by the 19:00 minute mark of the first half, and then didn't set foot back on the court until 2:42 was left in the second half. "Fastest I've ever taken someone out," Coach Knight proudly stated as he paused the game film at the exact point when he was taking me out of the game.

Coach then began to play the game film in super-slow motion. With his eyes on the giant projection screen, he smirked, *"Adios, m_ _ _ _ _ r f_ _ _ _ r. The only thing you could have done better was just turn left here as you run to the bench"* (a turn that would have sent me marching straight into the locker room rather than to our bench).

I truly believe that everything Coach Knight said and did during my three-plus years at Indiana was because he believed all of it helped make us better basketball players and a better team. The message may not have reached some players who were too distracted by the bad words and the loud voice, but if you focused on the root of it all, you would find that what he said was meant to motivate you and toughen you. Hoosier players who understood this derived countless benefits from their time playing for Coach Knight. Players who didn't understand or embrace this approach looked for the first exit ramp out of the Indiana basketball program. Coach Knight wasn't in the business of tailor-making his motivational techniques to suit each individual player's personality. He had one way to communicate that he had found to be quite effective for decades. Players needed to understand this very early on or they would never be able to get past the "how" part of Coach Knight's words and mine the benefits that lay within the "why."

We've all seen those highlight montages of Coach Knight that ESPN and other sport shows roll out from time to time. Of course, rare is the case when one of these montages show him calmly diagramming a play in a huddle or giving his team an encouraging clap of his hands. For most sports shows out there, it's become a paint-by-numbers exercise when it comes to doing any kind of Coach Knight highlights package: they run the chair-toss footage from 1985, throw in a sideline shot of Coach Knight hollering at an official, add a couple of entertaining press conference quotes of him poking fun at the media, and finally add a few clips of referee Ted Valentine trying his best to get under Coach Knight's skin (while at the same time acting like he's the reason people bought a ticket to the game). Just like that, you have your standard Coach Knight video crutch that most sports shows lean on for every story that involves Coach Knight.

The image that most of the media lazily paints of Coach Knight's last decade at Indiana is of a coach who "lost touch with today's players" or who hung on even as "the game passed him by." These always seem to be the go-to, default descriptions of Coach Knight's coaching ability during the final act of his Indiana tenure.

The *Denver Post*'s Mark Kiszla echoed the thoughts of many in the national media when he wrote the following on September 9, 2000, the day before Coach was officially dismissed: "The game has passed him by. With his Hoosiers pushed out of the big picture, Knight is caught in the shadows of a once-brilliant career."

Kiszla was correct about Coach Knight having to live in his own shadow. His achievements from 1971 to 1990 placed him at an elite level, reserved for only the greatest basketball coaches of all time. If you accept that, then of course it's going to be impossible to live up to such a rarefied standard consistently. Ask Tiger

Woods today how it feels to try to live and work in the shadow of the 1999–2005 Tiger. Coach Knight set a standard early that made it tremendously easy for later critics to say that he had lost his ability to coach at a high level and that his teams weren't able to compete against the best anymore.

To show the absurdity of saying that the "game had passed Knight by" over his final years at Indiana, let's make a brief comparison between Coach Knight's final decade at Indiana and the last ten full seasons that Bo Ryan had at Wisconsin.

Bo Ryan's record at Wisconsin from 2006 to 2015 was 264–88 for a .750 winning percentage. Coach Knight from 1991 to 2000 was 231–92, a .715 winning percentage. During his last ten years as coach of the Badgers, Ryan's teams achieved an AP Top 10 ranking six times. In Coach Knight's final ten seasons at Indiana, his Hoosier teams achieved an AP Top 10 ranking eight times (including three of his last four seasons, 1997, 1999, and 2000). From 2006 to 2015, Ryan and Wisconsin won two Big Ten titles, made three Sweet Sixteen appearances, and reached two Final Fours (the last Final Four appearance resulting in an NCAA runner-up in 2015). Coach Knight's teams won two Big Ten titles and made two Sweet Sixteens, one Elite Eight, and one Final Four from 1991 to 2000.

I don't make this comparison to diminish. Until his retirement in 2015, Bo Ryan was a dominant coach in the league that Coach Knight himself dominated for a quarter-century. As great as Ryan was and as good as his teams were, his record does not place him in the same echelon of coaches as Coach Knight. The comparison here shows how high the expectations became for Coach Knight in the wake of his eleven Big Ten championships and three NCAA championships. The media's preoccupation with what his later teams didn't accomplish rather that what they did paints an unrealistic and inaccurate picture. You aren't going to find any articles saying that "the game passed Bo Ryan by" for a simple reason: because his record and teams' performance show it hadn't. In another *Denver Post* article by Mark Kiszla, this one from 2014 ranking the top college coaches in America, Ryan was described as being "as good as any coach in the country. At any level." He certainly was. And you know what? The guy whose "declining years" stack up well beside Ryan's record wasn't bad either.

Yes, Coach Knight's teams had four first-round exits from the NCAA tournament in his last six years at IU. But does anyone think those early exits happened because Coach Knight didn't understand the game or forgot how to communicate a game plan to his team? That's patently absurd. Take the last of those first-round exits, from 2000. His Hoosier team that season beat three of the year's Final Four teams—North Carolina, Wisconsin, and eventual champion Michigan State. A one-game sample size from the NCAA tournament does not yield definitive results; a lot of factors can weigh heavily on a single game's outcome. And that was clearly the case in 2000: Coach Knight lost his second-leading scorer and leading rebounder to a knee injury in the first few minutes of that season-ending NCAA tournament loss to Pepperdine. For too many members of the media, predetermined negative feelings about Coach Knight outweighed nuance and actual statistical evidence, resulting in the ridiculous criticism that he was no longer a great coach.

I really don't mean to pick on Mark Kiszla. His article about Coach Knight was the first one I found after googling the phrase "Knight game passed by." But as fate would have it, the two articles I have mentioned here by Mr. Kiszla illustrate my point in comparing Coach Knight's "decade of failure" with Ryan's lauded ten-year run. The first article, about Knight at the time of his firing, was titled "Indiana Must Wake Up from Knightmare." The second was headlined "Bo Ryan Knows Coaching and Lessons of Life as Wisconsin Boss," and it opened like this: "Let me introduce you to college basketball's invisible genius. His name

Knight Lines

Where are your priorities going to be?
Some of you get all wrapped up with everyone
on campus patting you on the a _ s!
I'd want to be remembered as a part
of the Indiana basketball tradition!

—Coach Knight

Sophomore year, 1/29/99

is Bo. Bo loves fundamentals more than you love Mom's choc-
olate-chip cookies fresh from the oven. Ryan is old school. And
there's one more thing: Bo Ryan of Wisconsin just might be the
best college coach in America" (see bibliography).

And that is why I find my eyes rolling every time yet another
blind-leading-the-blind pundit espouses the same old tired, re-
cycled opinion about how Coach Knight lost his ability to coach
the game of basketball over his last decade at Indiana. And I
hope every member of Hoosier Nation reacts the same way I do.

I'm not saying that anytime someone does a story about Coach
Knight it needs to be all puppies and giggles. His outbursts and
legendary press conferences certainly need to be part of the overall
portrait. But his negatives shouldn't cover the entire canvas. Sure,
a large part of the reason that the media presents Coach Knight
this way is because he embraced the tell-it-like-it-is, shoot-from-
the-hip, old-school drill-sergeant image to a large degree. Thus
it's no surprise that his TV image is what it is today. The media

portrayal of Coach Knight has also been aided by the fact that he has chosen not to publicize many of the good works he has done through the years. Of course if there were video of Coach Knight doing great charitable acts, that footage might never see the light of day at most national media outlets, where they would rather show a chair being thrown for the umpteenth time. There definitely wasn't any video of the scene I witnessed after a brutal home loss to Ohio State. Just minutes after Michael Redd and Scoonie Penn led the Buckeyes to a crucial Big Ten victory in Assembly Hall (and then led their team to center court to dance on the state of Indiana logo), I saw Coach talking with a father and his son in a hallway near our locker room. I saw Coach down on one knee giving encouraging words of support to the small boy, who had recently suffered such severe burns that he needed to wear special protective clothing on much of his body. I wish more people could have had a chance to see this side of Coach Knight.

And I'm glad now that I have a chance to share how Coach helped out a family near my hometown in Tennessee not long ago after they had suffered a tragic death during a terrible winter storm. At that time, when I called to ask for Coach Knight's help, it had probably been a year and a half since I had last talked to him, yet his response was immediate and greatly helpful for the family in need. If I have personally experienced several stories like these involving Coach Knight, just think of how many more players, managers, and fans have probably experienced this same side of him as well.

I've said it before and I'll say it again: I hope everyone has a chance to know what it feels like to have a person believe in you to such a degree that you are pushed to achieve goals you didn't know you could reach. In all honesty, I don't think Coach Knight really gives a flying rip about who knows or doesn't know about the good things he does for past players and current strangers. Coach once made a point to have us write down in our red notebooks the following:

Intelligence and effort establishes *something*.

I think that today most of Coach Knight's former players are thankful that he used his talents and his work ethic to teach us how to play the game of basketball while establishing something that can never be taken away from any of us: a feeling of pride for being part of the Indiana Hoosiers family.

Acknowledgments

Thanks to my wife, Kasey. Kenner, Kooper, and Kyler are fortunate to have you as a mom.

Thanks to the Charlotte Hornets for drafting me—*and* for cutting me! Just a few months after being cut I was back in Tennessee working out at the Freed Hardeman University campus, and it was then and there I met my future wife.

Thanks to the Doyle family and the Kirk family for always being there for me. Thanks, Tony, for all the clippings and videos.

Thanks to Judy Varner (a great spell/grammar checker!) and Karen Fozzard (a great listener to all my complaints!).

Thanks to Mrs. Barbara Kirk for the example you set and the joy and strength that you have provided for Granddad and our entire family.

Thanks to the IU boosters for those envelopes of cash in my mailbox after every Big Ten victory . . . Just kidding! (I *almost* had you there for a second, didn't I?)

Thanks to Arthur Hitt for being such a great friend to me and my family.

Thanks to John and Ashley Carroll (thanks for all the good advice, Ashley!).

Thanks to Bruce Slatten for being a great coach to play for in high school.

Thanks to Cory Brown, Chris Jones, Blake Warren, Mitchell Rhodes, Phillip Carroll, Chad Marrs, Dan McEwen, Josh Warren, Shannon Hamm, Barton Coble, Clay Pope, Ben Mercer, Nick Coble, Josh Walker, Kenny Tohn, Troy Himes, Adam Trull, and Jeremy Hester for being a part of our 37–0 state championship team in 1997.

Thanks to the 1994 upperclassmen, Brad Cotham, Bryant Rhodes, Joe Gray, and Michael Clark, for setting the tone my freshman year for four straight state tournament berths.

Thanks to all the players that I've coached, especially those on the 2011 and 2012 Final Four teams, and my assistant, Cody Warren (I wish you had taken over as assistant coach in 2011).

Thanks to Tim Garl for your help through some tough days in college (and for putting up with Dane Fife for four years!).

Thanks to my good IU friends: Nicole Kelly, David Pillar, Brandon Sorrell, Ted Hodges, Jerry Hickey, the Buhers, Jill Cooley, and Betsy Pharion Stewart.

Thanks to Mike Lewis and Tom Geyer for making that trip down to Tennessee in 1999.

Thanks to "The Codgers" for coming to the golf course and getting beat on a regular basis by "The Bombers."

Thanks to Brent Hinson, Daniel Richardson, Alec Richardson, and Barry Cunningham for keeping my "Bombers" teammate, Caleb Dunkle, grounded and out of trouble.

Thanks to all my fellow teachers in the Perry County School System.

Thanks to all the great assistant coaches I've had that have put in countless hours helping me on the court and in the film room.

Thanks to Buzz Kurpius for all of her help while I was at IU.

Thanks to Gil Webb, who gave me the opportunity to coach at my alma mater, and to Eric Lomax for continuing to give me that opportunity.

Thanks to all the Perry County Ryder Cup players.

Thanks to Eric Hampton and all the GSC tour members for the great golf events.

Thanks to Dan McEwen and Josh Warren for all the late night basketball battles at the Lobelville Elementary gym when we were in high school. There was nothing like calling up two friends at 11 PM, knowing they would be ready to go to the gym and play until 2 AM.

Thanks to John McEwen for "not doing that kind of work anymore."

Thanks to David Lee and Bucky Haskins for all the one-on-one battles (Bucky, you're definitely one of the best 1,500 shooters I've ever seen!).

Thanks to Lance and Sandra Foster for raising a daughter who's a great Christian wife.

Thanks to the '50s and '70s Perry County teams that established a basketball tradition.

Thanks to Steve and Mitzi, Rick and Cindy, Matthew and Kara, Trent and Lori, Aaron and Cassie, Jamie and Kara, and J. C. and Bridget for all the fun game nights.

Thanks to Dane F., A. J., Mike L., Jared J., Calbert C., Jeff O., TK, Bryce D., Bob H., Coach Izzo, and Coach Crean for their time and kind words.

Thanks to Sarah Jacobi and IU Press for all their help and for the opportunity to tell my story.

Thanks to all the members of the Linden Church of Christ.

Thanks to the Indiana Hoosier basketball fans, one of the most incredible fan bases in all of professional and college athletics.

Thanks to Chad Marrs (even though he's a Texas Rangers fan). It's a rare thing to have a best friend who stays your best friend from kindergarten until this very day.

Thanks to all Perry Countians; it's been a blessing to grow up in P.C.

Thanks to Coach Knight for getting the most out of me on the basketball court.

Thanks to my mom, granny, and granddad for their time, teaching, and trust.

Above all else, I thank God for all the blessings that have been in my life.

"I can do all things through Christ who strengthens me."
—Philippians 4:13

Bibliography

Belmont, Jon. "Bobby Knight Continues to Fight." ABCnews.go.com, September 12, 2000.

Broussard, Chris, "Well-Drilled Indiana Overwhelms Seton Hall in Opener." *New York Times*, November 8, 1998.

Dufresne, Chris. "All He Wants Is a Little Respect." LATimes.com, September 9, 2000.

Ewell, Christian. "Second-half Rally Sends Kent State to Upset of No. 4 Seed Indiana." *Baltimore Sun*, March 16, 2001.

Hilburg, Alan, and Falkner, David. *Russell Rules.* New York: New American Library, 2002.

Hutchens, Terry. "Fife on Knight's Final Team Meeting. A Unique and Special Moment." USAToday.com, September 10, 2010.

"Indiana Keeps Coach Knight with Sanctions." CNN.com. May 15, 2000.

"Indiana University Basketball Coach Bob Knight Fired." CNN.com. September 10, 2000.

"Indiana vs. Kent State." USAtoday.com. March 16, 2001.

Katz, Andy. "Poor Shooting Plagues Chicago." ESPN.com, June 9, 2001.

Kiszla, Mark. "Bo Ryan Knows Coaching." DenverPost.com, March 28, 2014.

Kiszla, Mark. "Indiana Must Wake Up from Knightmare." DenverPost.com, September 9, 2000.

"Knight Says Goodbye to IU, Students." Amarillo.com, September 14, 2000.

Leung, Diamond. "Michigan State Assistant Dane Fife Returns to Indiana." Mlive.com, February 28, 2012.

McCauley, Janie. "Basketball Coaching Great Pete Newell Dies at 93." LATimes.com, November 17, 2008.

Rabjohns, Jeff. "Man behind Bob Knight Firing Says Incident Overhyped." *Indianapolis Star*, September 10, 2010.

"Ron Felling vs. Bob Knight." WTHR.com, March 9, 2015.

KIRK HASTON was a member of the Indiana Hoosiers basketball team from 1997 to 2001, including Bob Knight's last three seasons at IU. Haston was an Associated Press All-American in 2001 and was also named to the All-Big Ten teams in 2000 and 2001. He was selected as the sixteenth pick in the 2001 NBA draft by the Charlotte Hornets. At the conclusion of his professional basketball career, Haston returned to his hometown in Tennessee, where he earned his Master of Arts degree in education and began a career in coaching and teaching at his alma mater, Perry County High School. During his tenure as head coach, the Vikings have twice reached the Final Four in the state basketball tournament. Haston and his wife, Kasey, currently reside in Lobelville, Tennessee, with their two sons, Kenner and Kooper, and their daughter, Kyler.